# Market Research

**Robin Birn and Patrick Forsyth**

MARKETING

04.09

- ■ *The* fast track route to mastering the use of market research

- ■ Covers key market research techniques, from asking the right questions and using statistics to analysing data and acting on the information

- ■ Examples and lessons from benchmark companies in publishing, consumer goods, brewing and other industries

- ■ Includes a glossary of key concepts and a comprehensive resources guide

The right of Robin Birn and Patrick Forsyth to be identified as the authors of this work has been asserted in accordance with the Copyright, Designs and Patents Act 1988

First published 2002 by
Capstone Publishing (Wiley company)
8 Newtec Place
Magdalen Road
Oxford OX4 1RE
United Kingdom
http://www.capstoneideas.com

CIP catalogue records for this book are available from the British Library and the US Library of Congress

ISBN 1-84112-194-0

Printed and bound in Great Britain

This book is printed on acid-free paper

Substantial discounts on bulk quantities of Capstone books are available to corporations, professional associations and other organizations. Please contact Capstone for more details on +44 (0)1865 798 623 or (fax) +44 (0)1865 240 941 or (e-mail) info@wiley-capstone.co.uk

# Contents

# Introduction to ExpressExec

ExpressExec is 3 million words of the latest management thinking compiled into 10 modules. Each module contains 10 individual titles forming a comprehensive resource of current business practice written by leading practitioners in their field. From brand management to balanced scorecard, ExpressExec enables you to grasp the key concepts behind each subject and implement the theory immediately. Each of the 100 titles is available in print and electronic formats.

Through the ExpressExec.com Website you will discover that you can access the complete resource in a number of ways:

» printed books or e-books;
» e-content – PDF or XML (for licensed syndication) adding value to an intranet or Internet site;
» a corporate e-learning/knowledge management solution providing a cost-effective platform for developing skills and sharing knowledge within an organization;
» bespoke delivery – tailored solutions to solve your need.

Why not visit www.expressexec.com and register for free key management briefings, a monthly newsletter and interactive skills checklists. Share your ideas about ExpressExec and your thoughts about business today.

Please contact elound@wiley-capstone.co.uk for more information.

# Introduction

» A dangerous environment

"Good research reveals things I didn't know. Indifferent research reveals things I already knew. Bad research concentrates on things I know not to be true."

*Richard Shaw, Shaw Research and Planning, quoting an anonymous advertising agency planner*

Everything about modern business seems uncertain. We live in dynamic times, change is the order of the day and management must proceed with care and consideration if it is to make any undertaking successful. Alongside this, perennial issues still dictate business success. Product or service quality, financial acumen, productivity, efficiency, staffing, utilization of information technology, and many more – all have to be well handled if success has a chance of following.

In addition there is the question of marketing. Simplistically, marketing is the process that "brings in the business," and this is certainly vital. Even the best product will not sell itself; indeed, marketing has a role not just in creating revenue but in creating products. So, business is a challenging undertaking and further hurdles exist.

## A DANGEROUS ENVIRONMENT

First, virtually all businesses exist in a competitive environment. *Competition*, direct and indirect, will undo your best plans if it possibly can. Certainly its activities create a "moving target," demanding that strategies be adjusted continuously. Increasingly, competition has an international dimension and this only extends the effect it has on your activities.

*Markets* and *customers* are volatile too. Markets are affected as much by fashion and fad as by economics. Customers are increasingly demanding, ever more fickle, and their loyalty to products and brands is harder to win, and then is more temporary than in the past. A host of external factors act on markets and affect customers' willingness to buy. These include: *economic* factors and what customers can afford, *political* factors and how markets are allowed to operate, *social* factors affecting how people live and therefore what their needs are, *technological* factors such as the rise of information technology, and *environmental* factors that may affect choice and regulation. All these things are dynamic – witness the pace of change in the area of computers and technology alone. Other changes may progress more slowly but they change things no less; think of the social changes wrought in western society by factors such as two-income families or children being born later in life.

The net effect of all this can be summed up in one word: *risk*. Business is an uncertain undertaking. For example, launch a new product (reputedly with a success rate of only one in ten) and the risk is all too obvious. In some businesses, with the long lead times and massive capital undertakings of, say, manufacturing an airliner, this effect is maximized. Management must assess risks in all its decision-making and, while there may never be one demonstrable, right answer, what is decided always matters and there may regularly be a great deal hanging on the decisions that are made.

Decisions are assisted by knowledge and in this context information really is power; and this brings us to the role of *research* in business. *Market research* is a technique – in fact a body of techniques – that provides information to assist decision-making in business. It does not remove judgment and experience from the process, rather it supports them by providing a better basis of fact – both existing and new. It can do a whole range of things, from confirming a suspicion to unearthing new, previously unthought of, facts. Sometimes this new information changes matters just a little, though maybe significantly. Sometimes it may reverse a situation. Always the intention is to add to the objective element of decision-making, to make it better informed and ultimately more likely to take business in the right direction.

At the end of the day market research, in all its forms, has one overriding purpose – *to reduce risk and thus increase the likelihood of success*.

# What is Market Research?

"The function which links the consumer, customer and public to the marketer through information – information used to identify and define marketing opportunities and problems; generate, refine and evaluate marketing actions; monitor marketing performance; and improve understanding of the marketing process."

*American Marketing Association's Dictionary of Marketing Terms (ed. Peter D. Bennett)*

Let us put research in context. Decision-making is central to carrying out managerial functions to make the planning and monitoring process work. Good decisions are taken on the basis of availability and use of relevant information. The information of most concern to marketing management comes from markets and customers, present, potential, and future, and concerns the shape, size, nature, needs, opportunities, and threats within the market. Market research is the means of providing them with that information.

## DEFINITION OF MARKET RESEARCH

A clear definition of market research is:

"The systematic problem-analysis, model-building, and fact-finding for the purpose of improved decision-making and control in the marketing of goods and services."

This implies that research is not just an information tool, it is a means of providing guidance to help improve the abilities of management within an organization, as well as a means of making a contribution to the management of the marketing mix. It can be used to help decide on: the marketing strategy required to meet the challenge of new opportunities; which market gaps to approach; and which are the key areas of interest for future marketing strategies. It can also be used for monitoring the effectiveness of strategies adopted.

## OVERALL PURPOSES

The two basic purposes of research are:

» to reduce uncertainty when plans are being made, whether these relate to the marketing operation as a whole or to individual components of the marketing mix such as advertising or sales promotion; and

» to monitor performance after the plans have been put into operation. In fact, the monitoring role itself has two specific functions: it helps to control the execution of the company's operational plan and it makes a substantial contribution to long-term strategic planning.

Simply stated, research covers all the "finding out" activities of marketing. The methods used may be simple, such as the completion of the customer satisfaction questionnaires that you find in hotel bedrooms. Collecting and analyzing these progressively indicates the views of guests. Alternatively, methods may be complicated: data being gathered by post, telephone, e-mail, or from face-to-face interviews with large numbers of people spread widely, maybe internationally.

Research affects the essential first stage of a marketing function – the identification of consumer needs – and can continue to update those views in different ways as things change over time.

Here, as so often with marketing jargon, we need to be very clear. The description "market research" is applied in two different ways. First, it is an umbrella term for a number of similar, but significantly different, types of research. Secondly, one of these specific types of research is itself called "market research." With that in mind there should be no confusion. What sits under the market research umbrella?

It describes five major types of research:

» *market research* – which, as an individual technique, investigates markets asking who buys what in what quantity;
» *product research* – this focuses on the product or service, asking: what is right and wrong with the products of the company, or part of them;
» *marketing method research* – examines aspects of marketing activity to see how well it is operating, asking whether communication, distribution, etc. are effective;
» *motivational research* – this looks at the way people think, asking about the basic reasons *why* people buy the products they do and what they feel about them; and
» *attitude surveys* – these focus on customers' perceptions of, and attitudes to, products and the companies who make them.

Like any other form of research, marketing research – this phrase best describes the portfolio of different kinds of research listed above – can only investigate *past* behavior. It is not possible to *research* the future. Research is of course very helpful in *predicting* future behavior, but research is essentially different from prediction; and this is something that must always be borne in mind. When attempts are made at prediction (e.g., political or election opinion polls, etc.) then serious errors can be made. The fact that research is not infallible, cannot simply unearth exclusively accurate facts, causes some cynicism. One researcher (quoted anonymously at a Market Research Society conference) said: "Good research reveals things I didn't know. Indifferent research reveals things I already knew. Bad research concentrates on things I know are untrue." The role of research, therefore, is to improve the factual basis on which forecasts and decisions are made. It must be made to work hard and accurately to focus on information that does help.

## THE ROLE OF MARKET RESEARCH

It is worth spelling out in a little more detail the range involved here. Market research provides information that assists an organization to define opportunities for product development and market strategy. It works by assessing whether marketing strategies are accurately targeted, and by identifying market opportunities or changes that are required by customers. Market research tends to confirm issues that are well-known in a market initially, but if planned well and effectively it will also identify new opportunities, market niches, or ways by which to improve sales, marketing, and communications activities.

The role of market research, therefore, is to reduce uncertainty in decision-making, to monitor the effects of decisions taken, and identify the performance of a company or a product in the market.

## SPECIFIC USES OF MARKET RESEARCH

To be more specific, we can list five key uses for market research, namely to:

» identify the size, shape, and nature of a market, so as to understand the market and marketing opportunities;

» investigate the strengths and weaknesses of competitive products and the level of trade support a company enjoys;
» test out strategic and product ideas which help to define the most effective customer-led strategies;
» monitor the effectiveness of strategies; and
» help to define when marketing expenditure, promotions, and targeting need to be adjusted or improved.

The variety of purposes listed above makes it clear that market research is not simply a "first check." It *is* useful ahead of any action, but it also provides a means of checking and refining views as operations proceed. Companies, especially those for which budgets always seem tight, who have selected one of these uses for market research are always concerned to make the research a worthwhile investment. Best results come when their marketing and sales planning is influenced by the results of research. In other words, when research pays for itself by providing a basis for change and improvement in operational matters.

## FURTHER POSSIBILITIES

The range of possibilities for research is considerable. To illustrate further, some of the regular and main reasons for using market research are as follows.

» To provide data on the market, or a market segment, and to discover whether the sector is increasing, staying the same, or decreasing in importance to customers.
» To obtain information to help to understand who the customers are, and the way in which they buy and use certain products.
» To evaluate customer service, assessing what customers feel about the services that they are receiving and their quality.
» To research customer attitudes and needs on a continuous basis to discover which product types are selling and where there are opportunities for new sales.
» To achieve better targeting, understanding what media and messages influence consumers to buy the products.
» To identify changes in the market that will affect how marketing must proceed in future.

These, and more no doubt, give a real insight into the possibilities. Market research can be central to the marketing process, it underpins the activity, grounding it in reality and helping give it the best possible focus.

## SUMMARY

The key things characterizing market research are:

» it is a means to an end and can help improve marketing effectiveness and reduce business risk;
» it encompasses a range of different kinds of research and these can be deployed to help in a variety of ways;[1]
» while research employs "scientific" methods (statistical techniques amongst others), it is not infallible; it provides guidance, and this supports and enhances the management judgment that is always necessary; and
» despite its ultimate fallibility, it is a valuable aid and many aspects of marketing can benefit positively from its help.

## NOTE

1 To reinforce the scope of research, especially in its broadest interpretation, the following is the definition of *marketing research* given by the American Marketing Association, which says it is the: "Function which links the consumer, customer and public to the marketer through information – information used to identify and define marketing opportunities and problems; generate, refine, and evaluate marketing actions; monitor marketing performance; and improve understanding of marketing as a process. Marketing research specifies the information required to address these issues; designs the method for collecting information; manages and implements the data collection process; analyzes the results; and communicates the findings and their implications."

# The Evolution of Market Research

"The supply of information has increased greatly. John Naisbitt (author of Megatrends) suggests the world is undergoing a mega-shift from an industrial to an information-based economy."

*Philip Kotler, marketing consultant and author*

The history of market research is itself interesting and paints a fascinating picture of the increasing complexity and scope of the technique as it has developed over the years. This chapter adopts an essentially "time-line" approach, therefore, and, give or take a year, spans a century, starting with the birth of the "father of market research," George Gallup, in **1901**.

## EARLY DAYS

» **1911**: The first documented market research department ("commercial research") was established for the Curtis Publishing Company, USA by C.C. Parlin. Over the next 10 years or so, most research was conducted by advertising agencies as an additional service to clients. Much was basic stuff, but almost immediately sophistication increased: for example, Daniel Starch, a pioneer psychologist, devised a method for measuring readers' recognition of print advertising in **1922**.

» **1930**: Raymond Rubicam sees psychologist George Gallup's article in *Editor & Publisher*, "Guesswork Eliminated in New Method For Determining Reader Interest," and invites Gallup to come to New York and start the first research department in an advertising agency.

» **1932**: George Gallup (whose mother-in-law was running for Senator in Iowa) conducted what was probably the first scientific political poll (correctly predicting her election!).

» **1932**: Daniel Starch, a pioneer psychologist, establishes a readership research program that, through more than 240,000 interviews, annually surveys the readers of more than 1000 issues of consumer and farm magazines, business publications, and newspapers. Also in 1932, market/commercial research was given its first official definition by the US Department of Commerce:

"The study of problems relating to the transfer and sale of goods and services between producer and consumer, involving relationships and adjustments between production and consumption, preparation of commodities for sale, their physical distribution, wholesale and retail merchandising and financial problems concerned.''

So, not surprisingly, a somewhat ''mechanistic'' definition at this time – with no mention of motivations and buyer psychology. However, one of the foremost marketing textbooks of the day called it:

''. . . the analysis and interpretation of sales data, the relation of actual to potential volume, the setting of sales quotas, the analysis of salesmen's territories and accomplishments,[1] the making of surveys of marketing expense and other cost studies, the testing of new commodities or new sales plans, the checking of the efficiency of advertising and sales-promotion efforts, the study of the attitudes of consumers and dealers toward the company and its products, the evaluation of the company's selling policies and products, and the gathering and analysis of information concerning many other special subjects.''

This would still make a good definition today!

» **The mid-1930s**: Saw the start of motivation research where clinical psychological techniques are applied to commercial problems.
» **1935**: George Gallup founds the American Institute of Public Opinion in Princeton, New Jersey. $3mn was being spent on research in the US market at around this time and its use was common in many areas of business and industry, a fact reflected by the formation of the American Marketing Association (AMA) in **1937**. Over the next 10 years expenditure grew to $12mn a year; market research was now a common technique in industry around the world.
» **1948**: ESOMAR, the European Society for Opinion and Marketing Research, was founded initially as the Society for Opinion and Marketing Research.
    The Market Research Society was founded.
» **1949**: Publication of the classical book *Statistical Techniques in Market Research* written by Robert Ferber. Still a sound read for all market research and marketing people today.

Robert Ferber was Research Professor of Economics and Business at the University of Illinois from 1948-57.

» **1950s**: During this period the development of market research was characterized by the use of orderly and rigorous scientific procedure and a very heavy reliance on quantitative techniques for deriving information about marketing opportunities and problems. Yet, at the same time, there was a growing awareness that traditional qualitative research methods were inadequate in providing a total explanation of consumer behavior. It was concluded that the reasons people gave for their actions, which conflicted with the available data, were *posthoc* rationalizations and that new techniques were needed to get nearer the truth. Researchers turned to the possibilities offered by clinical psychology and motivation research to extend their understanding of consumer behavior. In addition, the first use of demographics was made by the US Government.

The first use of projective techniques was in 1958 by Mason Haire of the University of California in the investigation of consumer resistance to instant coffee. The development of extended interviews amongst *groups* of respondents (now known as *focus groups* or *group discussions*) to counter the inhibition that respondents felt when alone with an interviewer. These new "manipulative" techniques brought their practitioners considerable acclaim and notoriety; they were widely published in best-selling books such as *Madison Avenue, USA* by Martin Mayer (1958, USA).

Despite the success of many motivational studies in providing ideas and stimulation for clients, there was a great deal of skepticism, and often valid criticism, regarding the validity and reliability of the methods. Some diagnostic tools were lifted from clinical psychology and applied to mass behavior without any real knowledge that such application was valid, and then prescribed as a cure-all for every marketing problem.[2]

» **Late 1950s–early 1960s**: Sharp reaction against motivation research and a corresponding significant increase in the popularity of large-scale quantitative research. New theories were also being developed on how advertising worked; new techniques sought to measure advertising effectiveness; computers allowed a rapid development in the ability to handle large sets of numerical data. Advertising research assumed a new importance with the growth in new media, particularly commercial television.

» **1961**: In the US, Colley produced DAGMAR – "Defining Advertising Goals for Measured Advertising Results." This was a systematic approach to advertising and referred to the sequential states of mind through which it was assumed consumers would pass "... from unawareness to awareness; to comprehension; to conviction; and to action." This emphasis on measurable, sequential advertising models led to the development of a number of techniques which claimed to provide a quantified measurement of an advertisement's future performance based on extensive pre-testing.

The popular view was that motivational or qualitative research had only a small role to play in helping to stimulate the generation of ideas and hypotheses but that it should not be considered reliable and should be followed by large-scale quantification (the quantitative $v$. qualitative schism continues today).[3]

» **1960**: (Canada) The national PMRS (Professional Marketing Research Society) was founded. It is a non-profit organization for marketing research professionals engaged in marketing, advertising, social, and political research.

» **1960s**: The use of quota research in consumer interviewing is introduced. Provided that the quotas collect a sufficient number of each of the key socio-economic groups (or any other relevant quotas), then problems are minimized. George Gallup, who pioneered in media research as well as in public opinion, instituted a survey in which, for example, a cross-section of Philadelphia was telephoned the day after an evening of television and was asked to recall the commercials on the prime-time shows.

» **1962–3**: Founding of the Industrial Marketing Research Association (IMRA)

» **1964**: Research by academics at Princeton and the University of Pennsylvania lays the foundation of the technique that will become known as "trade-off analysis."

» **Mid-1960s–early 1970s**: The widespread belief that all important aspects of advertising were ultimately quantifiable was increasingly questioned – results were often difficult to reconcile with reasonable judgmental expectations about particular advertisements and campaigns. The result was an inevitable antagonism between people who created the advertisements and those that researched them.[4]

Advertising theorists examined the work carried out by Gestalt psychologists on perception. The concept that consumers were likely to perceive advertisements as a whole, using only the minimum of cues and symbols, had important implications for advertising pre-testing research, which had tended towards the isolation and scrutiny of different parts of an advertisement (there was a paper on the same topic at the MRS conference in 2000 – the argument is perennial).

Buyer behavior also began to be studied rigorously, such as the work by Ehrenberg (1966). At the same time, a great deal of experimental research work was being carried out into the concept of "brand personality." Qualitative research had suggested that successful brands were received as a totality with a "unique personality" – the implications for research methodology were spelt out in *What Is A Brand?* by S. King.[5]

As a result, the techniques which attempted to measure advertising effectiveness began to be discredited and the pendulum swung back towards qualitative advertising research techniques.

» **1965**: Theodore Levitt publishes his book *Industrial Purchasing Behaviour*,[6] a seminal work about why, and how, people buy.

» **1969**: Export Marketing Research scheme was introduced by the Government to assist British industry in overseas marketing research.

» **Early 1970s**: Declining response rates to postal questionnaires are experienced, leading directly to an increasing and more widespread use of telephone interviewing. Telephone interviewing is widely used in Sweden and Switzerland, for example, where more than 88% of households have a telephone. In other countries, for example France and Germany, researchers remain skeptical about the use of telephone interviewing at this time.

» **1973**: Sophistication increases further from this point on. Discussions around the industry make this clear. For example: an IMRA (Industrial Marketing Research Association) annual conference paper on "Recent Developments in Consumer Research Techniques and Their Application to Industrial Products" includes a review of the potential use in industrial marketing research of a new model of purchasing behavior, and theory of predictive research, being used in consumer research called the "Trade-Off Model." People are asked to rank products representing trade-offs between pairs of attributes; analysis uses the data-processing technique of Conjoint Analysis. The ability to use the trade-off model for market simulation and prediction means that it is likely to become a very useful tool to the new product planner, as well as to those involved with ongoing marketing problems.

Paper published on "A Practical Guide to the Use of Computers in Industrial Marketing Research." The development of high-speed computers has enabled more effective processing of data and has provided a problem-solving tool. Includes a description of a punched card (80 columns, each with up to 12 positions) and how to write programs to analyze the data. Also, the ability to apply statistical tests – such as the analysis of variance, t-tests, and chi-squared tests – involves tedious calculations that were possible before but are easily handled by a computer. The start of databases for sampling purposes. The use of techniques such as curve fitting, time series analysis, and exponential smoothing for the analysis of past sales/marketing data and forecasting.

» **1975–6**: Over 50% of UK households were estimated to be on the telephone in 1974–5. Telephone ownership is skewed towards the higher social class and upper income groups; telephone owners are more likely to own consumer durables and to live in the richer areas of the country. The argument for telephone research is that this bias can be allowed for. The case is that the telephone deserves its place in the consumer researcher's repertoire alongside the existing techniques of personal and postal interviewing; it has too much potential to remain a back number. The estimate is that 5% of telephone subscribers are unlisted (cf. around 20% in the US). So randomized dialing is not considered to be necessary in the UK. The first centralized telephoning facility is operational in London. Computer-assisted telephone interviewing (CATI) is possible.[7]

» **1981**: The trends in the use of particular techniques are shown by any examination of what the various professional bodies are discussing at a specific time. For instance, in this year the Market Research Society annual conference addressed the pros and cons of computer assisted telephone interviewing (CATI).

» **1982**: Mass interviewing techniques spread; an article published in the Netherlands is typical: "In Europe today, the use of telephone research techniques is becoming widespread and widely accepted as a really practical tool for today's market researchers. This is due to the steadily increasing levels of telephone penetration and the continuing non-response rates which are now a feature of face-to-face interviewing especially in large urban areas." The article goes on to talk about the "new computer-steered telephone interviewing system" which has been set up in the Netherlands; it has been used in the US for a number of years.[8]

» **1983**: US mainly uses random digit dialing; UK mainly uses telephone directories. US household telephone penetration is around 95%, rising to 100% in some states, but about 25% of homes are unlisted. In the UK the household telephone penetration is 80–85% but only an estimated 7% are unlisted. Whilst CATI is covered it is seen as a thing of the future, rather than as a current technique.[9]

» **1984**: The Data Protection Act received the Royal Assent on 12 July 1984. It represents the UK implementation of the Council of Europe's Convention for Data Protection and has had a profound effect on the conduct of market research ever since.

» **1986**: A sufficient proportion of American households had at least one telephone to make telephone interviewing a viable and substantially less expensive alternative to the standard in-person method. Such relationships between social behavior and methodology are common. By the end of the 1980s, the vast majority of Gallup's national surveys were being conducted by telephone. As we move into the 1990s, telephone numbers are being dialed automatically to create the necessary samples for consumer research.

## THE LAST DECADE

» **1990**: An advertisement by RSL (Research Services Ltd), now IPSOS, publicizes "the first national CAPI fieldforce" (computer-assisted personal interviewing) in the UK.

» **1992**: Founding of CMOR – Council for Opinion & Marketing Research – in the States. It is a grouping of organizations and corporations committed to protecting and promoting the integrity of the research process. CMOR supports programs that ensure access to consumers so that respondent co-operation in research remains healthy and vibrant.

» **1995**: (Europe) Data protection and data privacy laws: 1995 European Directive, a key directive, implemented in the UK as the 1998 Data Protection Act.

At around this point a great deal of additional activity is being generated around the link between the information technology revolution and market research, for instance, in 1995, Mehta and Sivadas set up a study which showed that e-mail could generate high response rates and similar ones to postal surveys. They also found it to be significantly quicker. They received a half of their e-mail questionnaires within three days, compared with three weeks to receive a comparable proportion of postal questionnaires. They found evidence of higher quality of responses and also pointed out the significant cost savings of the method (mainly for convenience of dispatch). At the same time, other surveys were showing consumer resistance to such methods.

» **1996**: First ESOMAR (European Society for Opinion and Marketing Research) paper on Internet data collection, published at ESOMAR/ EMAC Symposium in November 1996: "The Use of the Internet as a Data Collection Method." The purpose of the paper is to show how the Internet can, and has been, used commercially to conduct research. It also aims to provide guidelines for future studies. The study was conducted as part of a project for the Henley Centre on Media Futures (1996). Even now this remains a volatile area, some people feeling that there are problems making research representative in this way, others determined to make it work and getting good results from it. It is the nature of IT that this whole area will doubtless remain a dynamic one.

» **1997**: Original online panels were developed in the US by Media Metrix. 10,000 people buying new PCs had a software meter installed in them to record where they surfed.

» **1998**: Pioneering work on "pop-up surveys" by Micael Dahlen on the Swedish Website, Passagen.

Market Research Society adopts a professional approach to exam-based membership.

» **2000 onwards**: Now market research is a fully fledged marketing technique. It has its own codes of practice, its own experts, and an ever-widening range of ways of going about its business. Factors that once posed questions – can we do this research by telephone? – have changed radically (most people have one in sophisticated markets). But technology brings new worries. For example, there has been increasing concern over "professional respondents" (that is, respondents who complete many surveys). In the UK there is evidence that the average housewife, who is interviewed for a telephone omnibus survey, does 11 surveys a year. Anecdotally we hear that 50% of all responses in the US come from just 4% of the population. Although this problem exists in the offline world it can be much worse with online interviewing. This is because there is evidence that some people are seeking out surveys to complete. There are a large number of Websites (such as www.surveys4money.com, www.doughstreet.com, and www.rewardsites.com) that tell surfers where to find surveys from which they can earn money or win prizes.

The simpler ways now coexist alongside some very sophisticated methodology, especially when research is into mass consumer markets. The future will continue to see changes, and just as long as society and consumer behavior changes, so will the methods that are used to chart its progress.

## NOTES

1 And they were salesmen; saleswomen are a more recent phenomenon.
2 The debate and "blind" use and promotion of the latest techniques continues to this day.
3 May, J.P., "Advertising Pre-testing Research – an Historical Perspective," *Quarterly Review of Marketing*, Winter 1978.

4 There was a paper on the same topic at the MRS conference in 2000.

5 King, S. (1970), *What Is A Brand?*, J. Walter Thompson, New York.

6 Levitt, T. (1965), *Industrial Purchasing Behaviour*, Harvard Business School, Boston, MA.

7 Source: ''The case for consumer market research by telephone'' by Snatch & Snatch, Garland-Compton, 1976.

8 Source: Inter/view Group, the Netherlands.

9 Source: Frey, J.H. (1987), *Survey Research by Telephone*. Sage, CA.

# The E-Dimension

"First get it through your head that computers are big, expensive, fast, dumb adding-machines-typewriters. Then realize that most of the computer technicians that you're likely to meet or hire are complicators, not simplifiers. They're trying to make it look tough. Not easy. They're building a mystique, a priest-hood, their mumbo-jumbo ritual to keep you from knowing what they – and you – are doing."

*Robert Townsend, American businessman and author*

Things have moved on a bit since the quotation above, but some truth remains in the sentiments expressed. "Computers" have been enveloped within a much greater area that involves a whole range of information technology developments and the whole world of the Internet and e-commerce. Market research is a complex business involving statistics, samples, and much number-crunching; it is a field that needs the help of the new technology and has been immensely successful in embracing it and using it.

Even an overview of what is going on needs a particular type of expert. The words in the rest of this chapter are from one such and I am grateful to David Walker, international director, new media at the firm of Research International for his contribution.

## FIRST BASE

Although the initial development of the Internet can be traced back to the late 1960s, it has only been in the last six or seven years that it has truly become a globally accessible medium. The Internet has, in effect, become a collection of virtual communities, all focused upon the pursuit or sharing of information.

Business organizations have woken up to the potential of this medium as the technology and its usage have broadened. The tremendous hype and publicity surrounding the Internet would suggest that no organization can ignore its potential. For many this is not true; the Internet may be no more than a marketing or promotional tool. Organizations that will truly benefit will be those that can operate or distribute their services over the new medium. Market research certainly falls into this category, with the Internet representing an exciting new method of collecting and distributing information.

A number of new online research tools have been developed (and are still developing) which allow researchers to conduct traditional types of research in new ways, as well as some interesting new approaches.

However, before looking at the range of options available, it is important to understand the unique issues that affect the ability to conduct research over the Internet.

## THE BENEFITS AND DRAWBACKS OF ONLINE RESEARCH

From a client and from a research agency point of view, online research can be very enticing, as there are a range of cost, speed, and quality benefits to be found. However, like all research techniques, online research has its benefits and drawbacks. Unlike others, however, these are changing constantly as the usage and application of the Internet change. First, we consider the benefits.

### The benefits of online research

» *Inexpensive research*: In comparison to face-to-face or telephone research, online costs are significantly lower, as there are no interviewers and minimal telephone charges to pay. It can even be cheaper than postal research, given huge reductions in printing and postage costs.

» *Objective responses*: As respondents are typing in their own responses, feedback can be considered totally objective; there is no interviewer influence.

» *Unintrusive*: Respondents complete surveys at their own pace, when they want, and this has potentially beneficial effects on response rates and the quality of answers.

» *Speed of response*: Experience shows that responses can be received and processed much more quickly than by traditional methods. The ability to contact large numbers of people quickly through an automated process can make collecting and reporting findings very simple.

» *Quality of response*: Compared to telephone, or even postal research, respondents give more articulate responses to open-ended questions. This may be due to the fact that when individuals type, they are more accustomed to producing structured and formatted output that is reviewed fully before they proceed to the next question.

» *Technical possibilities*: Given developments in Internet technology and more and more respondents with high specification computer equipment, there is the possibility to use sound, graphics, and even video in some instances, expanding the possible research applications.

» *International research*: There are no international boundaries and so questionnaires can be completed as easily on the opposite side of the world as at a more local address.

» *Automation*: Data is collected in a pre-defined electronic format and so there is no need to re-enter responses manually, making considerable cost savings. Reporting can even be produced "real time," allowing anyone anywhere in the world to access the latest results of a survey.

## The drawbacks of online research

The drawbacks of the online approaches relate largely to sampling and sample control issues. However, as usage of the Internet continues to grow rapidly, some of these issues may be overcome in time. At present, key concerns are as follows.

» *A narrow target audience*: The types of individuals that are using the Internet have an obvious effect on the scope of research that can be conducted at present. Internet usage will vary significantly from country to country. Internet users may not be representative of the population as a whole, being perhaps more technically literate, affluent, or even male!

» *Identifying Internet users*: Accessing lists of Internet users to contact can be difficult. Random sampling is not always possible, as there are no equivalents to telephone directories, door-knocking, or street interviewing on the Internet – privacy is sought and generally respected. To identify our sample we may have to use pre-recruited sources such as panels or pre-defined lists.

» *Understanding the sample*: Knowing who exactly is participating in research can be difficult. E-mail addresses alone also give little indication as to the type of person using it. Identifying and controlling samples of Internet users is therefore a difficult process and needs to be addressed on a project-by-project basis.

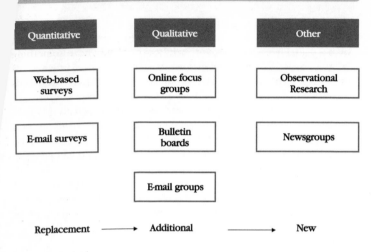

**Fig. 4.1**  Online research techniques.

but the Internet itself offers new research opportunities. The ongoing development of the Web will create new techniques over time. Two such approaches are highlighted in Table 4.3 as examples of using the Internet for new information.

## THE WAY AHEAD?

Despite some of the restrictions of the online techniques, there can be no doubt that these research methods are here to stay and that they are becoming increasingly effective as the user base of the Internet increases and as the speed and infrastructure of the system improve. As more users may move to high-speed broadband or cable for their access, many of the technical problems currently restricting these methods will be improved. Improvements in software development will also lead to a "new age" of electronic questionnaires, which will be even simpler to design and transmit if required.

The potential for research companies is substantial, particularly if one compares this method to postal or telephone research. There will be substantial cost savings, faster and improved response, and the

» *Technical restrictions*: The ways of accessing the Internet and varied. Some Internet users may be using high-speed over a digital telephone network whilst others may have son far more basic. With different degrees of access the "performan online research will vary between different users. Download s for surveys, and even look and feel, may vary from user to user.

» *Encouraging response*: As more and more online research is c ducted, respondents are becoming increasingly selective about th participation. Indeed, some consumers may be paying to participa in an online survey through Internet subscriptions and call charges Encouraging response then becomes an issue and it is now important to provide suitable incentives for consumers to respond (either financial or otherwise). These incentives can reduce cost savings on a project and could potentially cause some skews in the type of people responding.

## WHAT ARE THE KEY ONLINE RESEARCH APPROACHES?

A wide range of both qualitative and quantitative research approaches are possible via the Internet, although in reality the focus of most expenditure is in quantitative research, where the largest financial savings are to be made.

Figure 4.1 illustrates the most popular techniques currently in use.

In general, most development effort has been put into those techniques that provide real financial benefits over traditional larger scale programs – techniques that act as a "replacement" or substitute approach. However, some online qualitative approaches allow us to conduct research where we may not have been able to before, acting as "additional" services, with some new techniques being created as a result of the Internet itself.

But how do these approaches work and when can we best apply them? Table 4.1 and Table 4.2 enumerate and elaborate on common quantitative and qualitative techniques.

### New approaches

As we can see with the approaches above, it is quite possible to transfer traditional research techniques to the online environment,

**Table 4.1**  Quantitative techniques.

| Technique | What is it? | When could you use it? | Issues to consider |
|---|---|---|---|
| Web-based question-naires | A questionnaire hosted on a Web page. Respondents are sent to the page to self-complete a survey. A survey tool that allows the presentation of questions to be controlled and interactive. | Theoretically it can be used for most standard quantitative research approaches, although the audience is limited to Internet users. | Questionnaire length (surveys over 15 minutes may be difficult). How do you send people to the questionnaire? By e-mail invitation? By pop-up window interception? By a link on a Website? |
| E-mail question-naires | Questionnaires are placed in an e-mail then sent to a respondent. The respondent completes the survey contained in the e-mail and sends it back. The Internet is used as a tool for sending the e-mail, rather than to collect data. | Typically when a respondent may have an e-mail address but no access to the World Wide Web. Generally for business-to-business research. | There may be technical problems with varying e-mail systems. Sending large attachments in e-mails may not be acceptable to some respondents. |

ability to widen the type of questions asked to incorporate stimulus material such as sound or video clips.

It may also not be just the computer that offers an online research channel. The new generation of mobile phones will allow faster access

**Table 4.2** Qualitative techniques.

| Technique | What is it? | When could you use it? | Issues to consider |
| --- | --- | --- | --- |
| Online focus groups | A form of online chat, where respondents gather in a "chatroom" and discuss issues raised by an online moderator. The discussion is live and respondents see comments raised by other participants. | For chat-literate users (e.g. teenagers). For geographically dispersed respondents. For sensitive topics where face-to-face contact may be an issue. | Although findings are generally the same as traditional qualitative groups, responses may be less detailed and the lack of body language makes emotion difficult to interpret. |
| Bulletin boards | A Website where questions/views are posted on a regular basis. Respondents are invited to visit the site and respond to the questions/views with their own thoughts. | For tracking feedback on a product/service over a trial period. For brainstorming or idea development over time. | How do you encourage respondents to visit on a regular basis? Moderation and monitoring of the board may be time-consuming. |
| E-mail groups | Questions are placed in an e-mail and circulated to a pre-defined group of respondents. Responses are collated and fed back to the group for further comment. | For audiences without Web access. For more "time starved" respondents. Typically used in academic and business-to-business research. | Controlling the volume of e-mails sent to respondents, as increasing e-mail volume becomes an issue. |

**Table 4.3** New approaches.

| Technique | What is it? | When could you use it? | Issues to consider |
|---|---|---|---|
| Observational research | An individual's Internet behavior is observed and recorded. Respondents are recruited to participate and online behavior is tracked using "cookies" or software installed on their machines. | Audience measurement of Websites. Identifying effective locations (for advertising or retail messages). | Respondents have to be recruited and incentivized individually. Given the vastness of the Internet, large research samples are needed to get accurate measurements of individual sites. |
| Using newsgroups | Newsgroups exist on the Internet as text-based discussion forums formed by individuals with similar interests. They can be used as useful sources of information through monitoring or even participation. | For feedback on specialized topics. As a means of contacting groups with niche interests. | Respondents may not be "typical" Internet users and are often more technically literate. Participation should be handled carefully and politely, as external interference or "spamming" is not welcomed. |

to the Internet. Indeed, in Japan there are already more consumers accessing the Internet through a mobile phone than PC and "m-research" (online research through mobile) is a small but rapidly growing phenomenon. Interactive television also offers opportunities for online research and new possibilities for reaching a broader audience.

A growing concern for market researchers in the online world, however, remains data protection and the difficulties in identifying research contacts. Without a large effective sample source, online research is likely to remain a limited, specialized technique. To address this, we have seen significant research agency investment in building online access panels. These panels are expensive to recruit, maintain, and incentivize but offer great opportunity for accessing a broader base of respondents. However, accessing a panel for research will come at a cost and we may well see that the large savings in fieldwork costs, experienced in the early days of online research, will be reduced as panel managers (and respondents themselves) look for some return on their investment.

## IMPLICATIONS FOR THE MARKET RESEARCH INDUSTRY

Although online research techniques have been around for some years, they still represent a very small percentage of turnover for the larger research agencies, albeit a rapidly growing one. That rapid growth will have implications for the traditional market research agency.

» The resources needed to conduct online research are minimal. The large field force and resources of a major research organization count for little when conducting research over the Internet. We may see some restructuring amongst the larger research agencies as Internet technologies are implemented across the organization, not only in data collection but in reporting, knowledge sharing, and general communication. Traditional researchers may be augmented by technical specialists, programmers, and Web designers as organizations integrate Internet into their business.

» As Internet usage grows, it will be increasingly important for executive research staff in all organizations to become aware of the online research alternatives and techniques. As the technology is constantly developing, training and knowledge sharing will become critical.

» Online research does not appear to offer a threat to traditional "nationally representative" consumer research in the short term but for how long will that be the case? As Internet penetration increases, will market research companies be able to justify field interviewers or will they revert to online or electronic data collection methods? Will the shape and size of these field interviewing divisions change dramatically as online research grows?

» Will the way that the industry handles research projects change over time? The Internet has made us all "spoilt children" – we want things faster and cheaper. Research clients have become more demanding and online tools may offer a solution. We may see a trend towards shorter surveys conducted more often; and surveys conducted across a range of channels (computer, mobile, TV) to access a broader base of respondents. Faster turnaround projects with simpler objectives may become the norm, driven in part by the use of technology and demand for speed.

## SUMMARY

It could be argued that as a research medium the Internet will never be comprehensive and will be ineffective for many types of research. This may be true at present, but then the same argument was leveled at telephone research not too many years ago. The truth is that there is a time and place for online research but it is now very much established as part of the market researcher's toolbox and is becoming increasingly popular.

The difficulty, though, is in knowing when and how to use this tool. With the demand for speed in business decision-making, it is very tempting to take an online approach wherever possible to get quick, inexpensive feedback. "Online research" itself has become a buzzword amongst clients and it is important for the market research industry to resist temptation and take a measured and sensible view in its application. Only then will we see the development of online research as a truly respected and trusted technique in its own right.

# The Global Dimension

"The impact of the globalization of business is so profound that it has been described as the second Industrial Revolution. Globalization not only means bigger businesses, but also more complex businesses. Understandably, this increase in complexity means the information needs of organizations are also more complex."

*V. Kumar, consultant and author*

Marketing operates on a global canvas. While some companies, of course, restrict their activities to their home market, more and more are involved, one way or another, in international markets. Big brands are truly global, the Coca-Cola symbol is reckoned to be the most recognized image in the world, and many big brand names appear world-wide. Indeed, a recent chairman of Unilever is reputed to have said: "The first question to ask of any brand today anywhere is *'will it travel?'*" He went on to say not only that ideally it should travel, but that it should be made to do so fast, before local or international competition caught up with it. Market research can set out to answer that question and do so in any market you care to name.

There are examples of products that have enjoyed worldwide success with no research whatsoever. One of the most famous examples is probably the Sony Walkman. Certainly a hunch can pay off, but it may not. But would even that success story have been greater if research could have identified the potential and more resources were put behind it early on? On the other hand, lack of research can allow disaster. In Switzerland, tens of thousands of jobs were lost in the years immediately following the introduction of the electronic watch, while companies did nothing because they knew that it "was only a passing fad," and were convinced that their wide international market would return to their traditional, high quality product. Customers only did so after they had embraced the new technology. Research could perhaps have prompted them to take defensive action much sooner, by identifying the real views of customers.

One clear advantage of international operations is that it allows the simplification of product ranges. If products sell well in 30 countries, is there the same need to keep adding new ones? There are global advantages to many aspects of business: in marketing, distribution, production, and purchasing – but all are dependent on setting up international operations. This is beyond our brief here, other titles in the series address this but discovering if a market is viable and attractive is not.

## THE DANGERS

The need for sound and accurate information and the dangers of assumption in its absence are made clear by failure. One example is that of washing machines. When Whirlpool Corporation decided to move into Europe they were the largest appliance manufacturer in the United States. They thought the European market was now broadly homogeneous, that warnings about its regional nature were being overstated and that a major player that was innovative and able to operate cost-effectively would do well in what was a large market.

Their launch was countered by other manufacturers, they captured only 12% of the market, and in the mid-1990s were laying off workers and restructuring more than once. Why was this? The market was – and is – highly regionalized. Different consumers in different countries were driven by diverse preferences. Others were matching these local differences, while Whirlpool sold their "standard" products.

This sort of case illustrates a simple point – markets are individual and we know about none of them by instinct or crystal ball gazing. Consumers are demanding and fickle; *asking* what they might want and checking out how a market works is fundamental to success. Research clearly has a role to play in defining and segmenting their needs.

## INTERNATIONAL RESEARCH

This can be defined as research that is conducted, either simultaneously or sequentially, to improve the quality of marketing decision-making as it affects one or more countries beyond the home market. Not least it is designed to assist set priorities and the allocation of resources between different markets. The international dimension is sufficiently different to make defining the differences between domestic and international research useful.

The fact is that different countries have different political, legal, economic, social, and cultural habits and characteristics. This makes it dangerous, as was seen above, to make assumptions, and difficult too to compare one country with another – in the classic situation of not comparing apples with apples.

The main behavioral factors that international research must address are as follows.

» *Language*: language differences can affect the research itself, and the product and its promotion (for example, with a brand name meaning something rude or inappropriate in another language – thus the Norwegian crispbread delighting in the name *Nora Knackers* is unlikely ever to do well in Britain, at least under that name).

» *Culture*: attitudes and patterns of behavior can be very different, not only in obviously different countries such as, say, England and Saudi Arabia, but also in some that seem similar. From a European perspective, Singapore and Malaysia seem similar, but there are some significant differences, and Hong Kong, perhaps thought of as another Asian market alongside them, is more than a thousand miles away and different again.

» *Ethnic origin*: there is an overlap here with culture, but ethnic origin itself affects the marketing of some products (e.g. hair care).

» *Climate*: different climates and different patterns of seasonality need to be borne in mind. Food products are influenced, so too are clothes, and product durability and shelf life will be different too.

» *The economy*: income, spending power, taxes – all differ. How much of the French love of wine is cultural and how much relates to the low cost (with little local tax imposed)? This is a dynamic element of any market.

» *Politics*: this affects things in a number of ways, particularly in levels of control and regulation (e.g. the safety legislation that relates to many products, from cars to medicines).

» *Religion*: this affects the law, diet (e.g. consumption of alcohol), even the days of the week on which business can be conducted.

» *History*: the way history has affected and influenced culture needs to be taken into account (e.g. years of English rule gave India a population, many of whom are fluent in English, which is certainly the business language and results in English language books selling well.

» *Marketing*: for all that global companies standardize things (e.g. there are few countries where you cannot eat at McDonalds) there are differences in how people shop and in the consumption of products bought. For example, whether a drink is traditionally drunk before or after a meal may affect its sales considerably.

More specifically in terms of conducting research, consider the following.

» *Geography*: this affects how accessible people are. A truly national survey is possible in small countries (e.g. Singapore or the Netherlands), whereas in others (e.g. the US or France) it presents problems.
» *Communications*: how people can be contacted will vary too. In the UK researchers can gain access to people's homes and offices without too much problem; in some other countries this is difficult.
» *Facilities*: market research is very sophisticated in the western world. If you want to convene a hall test or a focus group or telephone 10,000 people within a week it can be done. This is not so wherever you may want to do research.

All these factors are just a further dimension to the differences that originate with factors such as age, sex, or socio-economic class. The various factors are not mutually exclusive and just add to the complexity of making a study valid.

Such factors can certainly cause difficulties. In his book *International Market Research*,[1] V. Kumar quotes a number of examples of culture clouding the issue:

» *product*: toothpaste manufacturer Pepsodent losing out because their promotion promised "white teeth" in Asian cultures where this was less than desirable;
» *promotion*: Braniff Airlines advertising in Mexico promised comfortable leather seats, but the chosen phrase was translated to offer people the opportunity to "sit naked"; and
» *place*: US food manufacturers identified that supermarkets and large stores were very differently regarded in the US and the UK, in the latter a local feel was necessary even for out-of-town shops, while in the States the link with anything local was not important.

## RESEARCH METHODS

Even in a "small" world there are many different ways of going about international research. The main ones include:

» a large organization doing things themselves from whatever local facilities they have in an individual country;
» a market research agency in the home country organizing everything – most usually through overseas offices or associates; and
» using an agency based overseas; many are virtually worldwide in their operation (e.g. Neilsen), others are regional, providing thorough coverage of a main market (e.g. such as AMI in Asia)

Whatever is done must be right when viewed from the end of the individual communications making up research. If housewives are being canvassed in Germany or food packing plants being researched in Japan or whatever, the research "on the ground" – that is making the telephone call, conducting the interview, or otherwise acting to obtain the information required – must be well-suited to that particular task. In other words, if interviews must be conducted in Japanese, in the evening, by someone with a particular knowledge of, say, coffee – then things must be organized to make that possible.

## SMALL IS ... POSSIBLE

All this speaks of large surveys. It is also possible to organize things more simply, indeed it may well be necessary to do so. For example, a company can send a member of their own staff to a country, though checking out the situation first – especially if it is a first visit, this may be vital – is not expecting to rush round and do everything in five minutes. When acting alone it is vital also to be objective; prejudices and assumptions must be left at home.

Here are two other examples which show different aspects of low-key and low-cost approaches.

» *A free dinner*: a personal recollection – on business in India I was asked by the manager of the large hotel in which I was staying to look at and comment on one particular aspect of the property: that of signage. The management team, not surprisingly, knew the hotel inside out. As a newcomer I was experiencing it for the first time, and like many of their guests had only a limited time to see and be tempted by their various revenue-generating features (i.e. restaurants, etc.). The result? Even after a careful inspection around the hotel, I missed the existence of one restaurant completely because the signs about it were few and poorly placed. My reward was a free dinner, their reward the opportunity to beef up the sign placement and increase business. Good thinking on their part and just as valid a form of research as any other.

» *Hand-holding*: this is a somewhat flippant way of describing a valuable way of combining research with action. There are consultants and firms in different markets who will act as what is effectively a temporary member of a client's staff. They will undertake a personal investigation of a market – one they know well, so they can tackle the job promptly and efficiently. Then they will move on to undertake specific follow-up tasks such as locating and setting up a deal with a local agent. All or part of this can be done in tandem with someone from the company for whom they are acting. This is very valuable and avoids any delay or mistakes that can occur during a first-time visit to a strange land. Many organizations can be found to work this way. One such is Gary Lim Associates in Singapore. Gary is an experienced marketing man and brings much more than simply research skills to the role. In this case, working with UK companies can be facilitated by an association with myself in the UK – an initial meeting can be held face-to-face in the country from which the project originates.

## BEST PRACTICE

Finally in this section we look at an example that spans the globe, and which also shows how research can be used to support specific aspects of the marketing process, in this case customer service. Most American airlines use continuous customer satisfaction surveys, both to gauge customers' reaction to and rating of their service, and to quantify the importance of the different areas of the airline's operation by using factor and discriminant analysis of all the attributes and the degree to which they explain the level of customers' satisfaction or dissatisfaction.

Many factors: delivery of bags at the carousel, waiting time for take-off, time taken reaching the gate on arrival, schedule reliability, and in-flight service, etc., are all measured. Survey results – about both themselves and competitors – are communicated internally so that everyone, including flight crews, understands how customers feel.

The research is thorough and ongoing. One percent of flights are sampled in the US and 10% of their international flights are checked. Two different questionnaires, designed to "turn intangible aspects of service into tangibles," are used. The first asks about marketing topics, that is to say, issues such as ticket purchase decisions, timing of travel, place of ticket purchase, length of stay at destination, purpose of trip, awareness of schedules, etc. The other focuses on customer satisfaction, investigating everything from ticket purchase through to check-in and on-board service.

Managers thus see continuous attitudinal data to make decision-making easier. Information brings a quantified element to bear on matters that are often less precise. As well as decision-making taking account of basis business statistics – *we are 5% above revenue target* – they also know if *customers are rating our reliability five points higher than our service target*.

This is not just research to provide an occasional burst of data. It is an ongoing measurement, designed to provide a continuously better way to make operational decisions. It involves many members of staff, is seen by many more, and provides an invaluable tool for those planning the airline's international operations.

## SUMMARY

When the markets contemplated are far away, be aware that:

» the risks attendant on all aspects of marketing are higher in an unfamiliar market;

» information is therefore vital, and thus time and resources should be made available to ensure that plans advance on a basis of firm, positive information;

» the cultural differences of both doing research in, and subsequently marketing to, another country should not be overlooked or under-estimated; and

» the right facilities should be lined up in order to do the research in a way that suits the organization, the location, and the information requirement.

## NOTE

1 Kumar, V. (2000), *International Market Research*. Prentice Hall, Upper Saddle River, NJ.

# The State of the Art

» Techniques of market research
» Data collection
» Communications, advertising, media, and the Internet
» Analysis and modeling
» Presentation
» Knowledge distinguishes successful companies
» Summary

"Increasingly, marketers are viewing information as not just an input for making better decisions, but also a marketing asset that gives competitive advantage of strategic importance."

*Rashi Gazier, consultant*

The role of market research is clear (see Chapter 2) – essentially it sets out to discover and analyze information that will reduce risk in decision-making, linked to how an organization relates to its markets and how it plans and implements its marketing.

The techniques and methodology that market research deploys are many. Their use demands specialist skills and, like so much in marketing, it is dynamic – not least, the techniques themselves are constantly developing and changing. Their successful use is, in major part, dependent on experience of both market research and the broader issues of marketing. Here the intention is to provide a short cut to obtaining that experience, and in this section a number of different factors are touched on briefly under a series of main headings that will guide you through the whole complex process. In this way, despite the restrictions of space, we can touch on all the key issues involved in research.

The arrangement is broadly chronological, starting with factors to do with preparation for research, and ending with the presentation of findings and how it can make decision-making less uncertain.

## 1. TECHNIQUES OF MARKET RESEARCH

The first heading takes us into elements that crop up at the beginning of the process.

» *Planning market research surveys*: Lurking behind most research surveys is a problem that needs solving (though this includes "positive problems" like seeking to find the best way to take advantage of an opportunity). At the outset of any study it is the researcher's job to determine what the problem is and show how it can be solved. The researcher must develop skills in taking a brief from the "problem owner" and translating it into a "proposal" for carrying out the study. In the proposal the researcher states the objectives of the study, the methods which will be used to meet the objectives, the timing, the composition of the research team, and the cost. This is true whether an organization is undertaking research itself or retaining a specialist agency.

» *Desk research*: There is no point in reinventing the wheel in a costly and time-consuming manner. If data exist, they should be used and not collected afresh. Desk research is the collection, sifting, and interpretation of published data. It plays a part in most surveys, even if only to use the known breakdown of the population to guide the selection of a quota sample. Elsewhere it may involve the researcher in delving in the library or searching online databases for information on market size and structure. This is an area where the ongoing IT revolution has created many new options (see Chapter 4).

» *Standards and methods*: Standards have had an increasing impact on the practice of market research. In the UK these relate primarily to the Market Research Society's Code of Practice (see Chapter 9). Standards do not define good methods, but they encourage quality. They are intended to be implemented at an organizational level, rather than being a matter for individual practitioners – but they need to be followed by practitioners in an organization.

» *Sampling and statistics*: Sampling is a worry for most researchers who are new to the business. The mathematical basis that allows small numbers to be researched with the confidence that they are truly representative of the population as a whole (whatever the group is) is vital to research. Understanding the rudiments of random sampling is necessary, even though in most day-to-day surveys the researcher may learn to trust a quota sample of interviews spread across the market. Without an appreciation of why and how different samples are selected, the researcher cannot claim to be undertaking a valid, scientific piece of work. Research must therefore be conducted in a way that brings specialized knowledge about this factor to the table.

» *Questionnaire design*: Good market research is about asking the right people the right questions. Not much more, and not much less. We all ask questions in our daily life. We all fill in forms, and are critical of them if they are the least bit ambiguous. In theory, questionnaire design should be easy, and yet it is one of the most difficult tasks to get right. Designing questions which draw out accurate information from everyone, which can be completed easily by the interviewer, that flow well and leave respondents feeling that they have contributed something worthwhile, should be the aim of all researchers. This is therefore an especially important part of any study.

» *Geodemographics*: Time was when survey samples were selected from a representative quota of the population based on sex, social class, and age. Over the last 20 years the technique has made it possible to link the characteristics of people with the neighborhoods in which they live. This has become a powerful tool in allowing researchers to infer certain types of behavior through knowing the geography of people's homes. Geodemographics gave sampling a new lease of life. Data from the 2001 census will give the techniques further development opportunities. This is clearly of most importance to research directed widely across the population as a whole; for an industrial company wanting to research buyers of, say, agricultural machinery of some sort, the identification of people to contact is less of a problem.

» *Quantitative research over the Internet*: The Internet has become a collection of virtual communities, and all are focused on sharing information. For some organizations the Internet may be no more than a marketing or promotional tool. For others, they will benefit from operating and distributing their services over the Internet. Market research is a service which now finds the Internet providing a new method of collecting and distributing information. As a result, Web and e-mail questionnaires can be useful tools to researchers. The sophistication of this area changes as you watch, as do the applications to which it is put. (Chapter 4 provides a comprehensive overview.)

## 2. DATA COLLECTION

The next area to consider is the part of the process that actually pulls together the raw data. There are a variety of different ways of going about this; they are not, of course, mutually exclusive, and a mix of methods may be used in many research projects. Some methods match very logically with a particular target audience. It may be so numerous that only low-cost methods are possible, or so difficult to contact that special – and more expensive – contact methods are the only way.

» *Quantitative research*: Quantitative research is that which supplies a number to anything that can be measured, indeed there is a large body of researchers who argue that measurement can be applied to anything. Quantitative research produces "hard" data which can be defended or challenged and which are more than just opinion. It is based on sizeable surveys which, in the main, use samples of upwards of 100 people. However, the well-rounded researcher does not see quantitative research as a technique that can stand alone. It is often appropriate to plumb people's opinions first using qualitative techniques before determining exactly what should be measured. The qualitative and the quantitative methods therefore are often best used together in this way, though it is always somehow easier to give findings credence when something measurable is involved.

» *Face-to-face interviewing*: The market research industry has been built around the core technique of face-to-face interviewing – in the street and in the home – and industrial research in the office. It is still the bedrock of many studies, as it allows the interviewer to use personal skills to elicit the information in a way that enhances accuracy. It also allows the showing of visual aids, smooths the interview, and allows deeper insights to be gained than through more mechanistic methods. In recent years, CAPI – computer-aided personal interviewing – has given the traditional technique technological advancement and efficiencies.

» *Telephone interviewing*: The telephone rose in popularity as a market research tool in the 1980s as it allowed interviews to be carried out speedily and under close supervision through central control. Now that almost all households have a telephone (and often more than one!), this means of contact allows the researcher to easily sample households anywhere in the country; indeed, it is a technique that can allow prompt contact internationally also, albeit at higher cost. Chapter 5 looks at research on international scales. It is not necessarily a cheap method, in fact it costs approximately the same as a street interview. CATI – computer-aided telephone interviewing – has enhanced the technique so as to increase quality and provide more detail from the interviews.

» *Postal Surveys*: Sending a questionnaire through the post must be one of the simplest scenarios. There is a certain prejudice about the use of postal surveys, a belief that the response they bring is usually inadequate. But this is perhaps only because they are frequently used in the wrong circumstances. They produce excellent results when there is a strong relationship between the respondent and the company carrying out the research. They are suited to testing opinion and sensitive subjects, and work best with closed questions. Case studies have been developed to show which approaches work best for maximizing responses. You will sometimes see a similarity between postal research and direct mail marketing techniques, in the sense that both are susceptible to minor differences influencing the response; for example, just changing a heading, adding further explanatory text, or providing an incentive to respondents makes a difference. Indeed I (PF) received a very nice pair of sunglasses from a motor manufacturer in the post this morning following my completion of a questionnaire for them some days ago.

» *Omnibus research*: Omnibus studies are surveys of the population or other selected samples and are run at regular intervals. They provide the facility for an organization to buy space for a limited number of questions in a large interview program. Because the cost of the interviewing and analysis is shared among a number of organizations, each contributing questions to the omnibus, it is a particularly cost-efficient means of collecting data. This is a technique which has seen an ever-expanding range of omnibuses covering all manner of target groups spring up over the years.

» *Panels and diaries*: A panel differs from an omnibus study in that it is a survey of the same people each time. In practice it is not always *exactly* the same people all the time as people drop out and need replacing. Care is taken to find replacement panel members with similar demographic characteristics. The questions that are asked of the panel are consistent so that results can be tracked over time. This provides reliable trend data on purchasing or on such things as television viewing habits. Such panels, and they exist all over the world, are usually sponsored by large media or consumer goods companies wanting to keep a check on movements in their target markets. The panel members keep records of their purchases and activities in diaries; that term is used here therefore in a technical sense.

» *Retail audits*: As the name suggests, retail audits take place at the shop or store. By checking the stock turnover at retailers the audit companies, which instigate this sort of research, produce accurate figures on the market shares of a wide range of consumer goods. The subscribers to the audits can then use the results to monitor changes in brand shares, and within the distribution routes through which their goods are sold, and in turn to adjust their strategies in the market-place to accommodate the latest situation.

» *EPOS*: EPOS stands for Electronic Point Of Sale. It describes a process carried out by scanning the bar codes at the check-out, typically at retail outlets. This allows researchers to measure quickly and accurately which goods have been sold and at what prices. EPOS is an extension of the retail audit. It is an excellent means of tracking product data as well as furnishing researchers with a basis for much predictive modeling.

» *Qualitative research*: In many studies researchers want to obtain a deep understanding of not just what is happening, but *why* and *how* something is happening. To achieve this the qualitative researcher works with small samples of people, sometimes on a one-to-one basis and sometimes in small groups. These are less like interviews and more in the nature of conversations or discussions, allowing observation of attitude and body language. They are long and unstructured and require considerable skill to draw out relevant information, and more to analyze the significant facts from them afterwards. Qualitative research can produce rich data, probing into people's unconscious attitudes, needs, and motivations. Because the samples are small, there is no attempt to measure responses.

» *In-depth interviews*: Using open-ended and unstructured interview guides, the researcher carries out in-depth interviews to "get beneath" the superficial responses. The in-depth interview permits the researcher to be flexible in the order and style of questioning so that avenues of interest and relevance to a particular respondent can be explored. This can be a valuable technique, but time equals money in all such contexts, so expenditure is increased.

» *Group discussions*: In a group discussion (or focus group, a phrase that has entered the consciousness of the general public through the use of them by political parties) between five and twelve people are led into an exchange of views by the researcher (who is called the moderator). The interactions between people in the group is used to flush out views that would not otherwise be raised in one-to-one interviewing. The group discussion is a widely employed technique for researching new concepts and guiding creative teams in advertising agencies. Group sessions can yield rich information, but they do require experienced researchers to direct them and make them work, and obtain true responses and not just the "party line." Here, too, costs can be high.

» *Hall tests*: There are many occasions in market research when it is necessary to have people look at (or touch or) taste a product. For all sorts of reasons it may not be possible for this to take place in consumers' homes. When this is the case, hall tests are set up. Target consumers are "recruited" from busy streets and invited to a nearby hall where the test takes place. A variety of techniques may be used in this context, but all have one thing in common: using the product itself as part of the inquiry.

» *Sensory evaluation*: Sensory evaluation is a tool to help the technical research and development teams design better products. It focuses on a small number of aspects of a product, such as the materials that are used in its manufacture, their quality, the shape of the product, and its performance in use. Data can be mapped to show where the product stands against consumer preferences and in comparison with the competition. Because the evaluation considers a number of variables, this type of new product research benefits greatly from multivariate analysis.

The profusion of techniques is obvious here, and these can be kept in mind as we focus for a few paragraphs on another dimension of research.

# 3. COMMUNICATIONS, ADVERTISING, MEDIA, AND THE INTERNET

The following is included just to give a feel for the broad scope of some research.

» *Advertising research*: Everyone knows the phrase, usually attributed to the chairman of Unilever: *I know half of my advertising is wasted, but I don't know which half*. It makes a good point and reminds us that for all the scientific method involved these days, marketing remains as much an art as a science. But what measurement can be done of areas of significant expenditure like advertising, must be done. Advertising research employs both quantitative and qualitative techniques. Large-scale samples are used for this purpose. Backing up the quantitative studies are group discussions or in-depth interviews which test the adverts or give creative teams in advertising agencies ideas for campaigns.

» *Researching TV and radio*: Broadcasting nowadays is a highly competitive business. The transaction from analogue to digital transmissions is revolutionizing the structure of broadcasting. Competition for audiences has been good for the business of audience researchers. The audience researcher can contribute his or her professional skills to identify the talent appropriate to the station, its deployment and promotion. Researchers working in this area need to deploy a wide range of research tools and do so in an area where practice changes very fast.

» *Peoplemeters*: In the past, research into television viewing habits was done by getting panels of people to record what they did in diaries kept in their homes. This method worked well when homes had just one television set and the family normally sat watching it together. Today television viewing is complicated by the many sets in homes, greater individual rather than group viewing, and the use of video recorders. Peoplemeters overcome these problems. They are electronic devices which monitor all the sets in the home – and the viewing on video recorders. They are "plumbed in" to the homes of people selected to go on the panel and provide accurate measurement of what occurs.

» *Packaging research*: Packaging is an integral part of many of the products we buy. It plays an important functional role in protecting the product, and it carries visual information describing the contents. In addition, it is a mini-advertisement actively playing a final role in merchandising and inviting consumers to buy. Packaging research is used to determine how well current or new packs actually work. In many cases straightforward questioning in the home or in hall tests will find out people's attitudes to packs and their design. However, other techniques such as tachistoscopes (which measure blink rate and are used to judge how much attention people give to things they see) are available and can show how rapidly the visual information on the pack is absorbed.

The examples here show how research can be focused on very specific aspects of the marketing process: the product, its packaging, as well as the behavior of potential buyers.

## 4. ANALYSIS AND MODELING

Just assembling a "pile of data," as it were, is of little value in its own right. The data need analysis, they need interpreting to make them able to play a proper part in decision-making.

» *Data analysis*: Data on their own have no value. It is the implications of data that really matter – what they show or suggest. This means that researchers have a responsibility to tease out only the data that are relevant to the objectives of the study, and to simplify them so that the user can quickly and easily see a pattern. The data must be presented in a form that the reader can understand and, hopefully, they will lead naturally to conclusions and recommendations. This part of the process may be automated and conducted largely by computer, but the job of setting up the required analysis is skilled and important. Only bad research collects large amounts of information and leaves it at that.

» *Modeling*: Computers have enabled researchers to get more out of their data than ever before. For example, programs now exist for testing the prices which people will pay for a product. They can show the degree to which consumers will trade off some feature such as quality or design against price. Simulated test markets can be set up. Missing data can be inferred by "fusing" together sets of data. Data can be analyzed to map or segment consumers to show their different characteristics or attitudes to brands. And the models can be used to forecast a course of action. This is an area of considerable complexity. As such, it may be beyond the remit of many small organizations, but technological change is making it more accessible all the time.

# 5. PRESENTATION

It may be an obvious point, but the nature of research makes the presentation of its findings an inherently important part of the whole process and worth a brief comment.

» *Presentation and report writing*: The final output of researchers' efforts is the presentation of their work – their findings. Presentations are the "day of reckoning" for researchers; a chance to make a mark for better or worse. Good presentations have a clear objective. They are short but to the point, with little time spent describing the method and more time spent on the findings and conclusions. The use of visual aids to communicate the data through charts and diagrams has become sophisticated, and the use of PowerPoint means good, clear information can be produced quickly and cheaply. While the personal presentation has impact, it is nevertheless ephemeral. The written report is more enduring and may be read over a long period of time. It is worth getting it right (it may come back to haunt its writer in times to come!). As with presentations, the same rules apply. The audience must be kept in mind and the writing style should quickly and clearly communicate the points, leading logically to the conclusions and recommendations.

This aspect is heightened in importance by the very nature of research findings. Most people cannot grasp complex figures and their implications instantly, and most find a clear graph easier to take a point from than a lengthy computer printout. It is possible, of course, for figures to give the wrong impression (as Benjamin Disraeli said: "There are three kinds of lies – lies, damned lies and statistics") and care is always necessary in the presentation of such information. In the case of research, information has been produced at the expense of time and money and it is obviously wasteful if its poor presentation disguises rather than enhances its value.

## 6. KNOWLEDGE DISTINGUISHES SUCCESSFUL COMPANIES

Let us put all this in context. The risks faced by businesses today have never been greater. Competition is fierce at every level of the market. Small businesses are likely to be funded by a family's life savings or expensive borrowing. The cost of failure can be very high for the entrepreneur and for their associates. Large businesses face the same risks except that there are more noughts on the figures. The cost of failure for the large business may mean redundancies, scrapped plant, and dire financial losses.

Success and failure in business is a consequence of making the right or wrong decisions. The right decisions are easy with hindsight; much more difficult when the conditions are unknown. It is a relatively simple matter to plan the production resources and estimate the financial requirement for a business. And yet both these plans must be based on understanding the needs of the market, and on whether customers buy the products and then become repeat buyers.

It is those market needs that are most often misjudged, assumed, or even taken for granted. Uncertainty about what the market wants, both now and in the future, is one of the most difficult problems with which businesses must cope. More than ever, decisions in business require robust information. If information on markets is a key to business success, it follows that the people who can supply it hold considerable power.

It is the role of market researchers to provide sound information to guide business decisions, set strategies, and monitor the implementations to give feedback on whether it has been successful or unsuccessful. And, one might add, it is the role of marketing people and senior management to demand or organize such information. The techniques available to researchers have been developed and polished, especially over the last three decades (see Chapter 3 for some history). There is no area where market research techniques cannot be used.

They are as useful in social marketing to probe why people drink and drive as they are to manufacturers selling alcoholic drinks; as useful to the government trying to obtain recruits for the armed forces as for theater managers trying to measure their audience's likes and dislikes. The skill of the market researcher is not just being able to apply a special technique, but also knowing which to apply and when.

## SUMMARY

While market research should not be seen as a panacea able to cure all business ills, it is a valuable asset in the battle to survive and prosper in the commercial world, indeed in any sort of organizational life. It should be remembered that:

» it is a complex, specialist technique which demands that the right mix of techniques is used in the right way (something that may also demand specialist expertise);
» it can assist – or rather its findings can – in the decision-making process, but does not replace judgment which is also necessary alongside the interpretation of research findings; and
» it is only ever as good as its brief; ask the wrong questions of the wrong people and it should be no surprise if the findings are neither reliable nor useful.

Good research is certainly useful. Lack of research, or bad research, can seriously handicap – and at worst cripple – an organization. But it should never be underestimated. Yes, some simple research is possible. Yes, simply ensuring you remain objective about your decisions and take into account all the salient, and available, facts is, in a sense, a form of research. But, as this section clearly shows, the implementation of a sound research study is a complex business. Only when it is done in the right way will its value be greatest. Then it is, for many businesses, not a desirable option – it is an operational necessity without which they are effectively operating with one arm tied behind their back.

# In Practice

"Learning without thought is labor lost; thought without learning is perilous."

*Confucius, Chinese philosopher*

"To manage a business well is to manage its future; and to manage the future is to manage information."

*Marion Harper, Jr*

Here we look at two different aspects of research in action. First there is a short overview of the structure of a typical research project and a description of how it is implemented. This puts much of the previous section in context and sets the scene for the second part of this one, which consists of a number of case studies showing more about how research works and what it can achieve.

## A RESEARCH PROJECT – AN OVERVIEW

There is a good deal of complexity about research, perhaps particularly in the area of methodology. However, the overall structure of a research project does follow a pattern and a snapshot of this helps put the process in context. The following encapsulates the process and does so for a project conducted by a market research agency (though things would not be changed so much by it being an internal project).

Six key stages are involved.

### 1. Objective setting

This is a necessity if the research is to have a clear focus and not get out of hand, either trying to look at everything or looking selectively and not at what will produce the information required. Objectives should always be: specific, measurable, achievable, realistic, and timed. It is as important to be clear on boundaries and what will *not* be done as on what is to be done.

With objectives clearly in mind, the next stage follows logically.

### 2. The brief

It is sensible to have a statement in writing that summarizes the project. This prevents misunderstandings, especially when a number of people are involved. The brief should state clearly:

» the objective, commented on above;
» the problem the research should address, or indeed the opportunity;
» what is known already about the issue being researched (and what is not);
» the business context in which the project will take place; and
» something about the method to be adopted.

## 3. Designing a research program

With an agency-conducted project this will be described and summarized in the research firm's proposal and normally follows discussions with them about the brief.

The possibilities and limitations of the program must be clear, and a typical proposal will set out:

» the background, referring to the reasons for doing the research, specific objectives, and the areas of information to be investigated (and indeed not included);
» the methods, or often the mix of methods, to be used (these may vary from telephone interviews to personal interviews). Here, too, there should be a clear description, if necessary, of the categories of people to be approached. Note that there is no one "right" mix of research methods for a project. It is possible – probable – that different firms pitching for work will suggest a different methodology mix, and suggestions need weighing carefully before a final decision is made;
» the timetable, like any project the stages and timings need to be set out; and
» costs, fees, and expenses that the agency will charge for the prescribed work (more than one quotation, as has been said, may sensibly be sought). Research can suffer from the wrong financial view: too high a cost may just be a firm over-engineering to inflate the profitability from a potential project, but too little being spent may render the scale of the project too small to be able to produce meaningful results.

## 4. Fieldwork

Then the right questions must be asked of the right people. An appropriate statistical sample may be needed and this will need to link appropriately to the methods to be used. The work itself (perhaps preceded by some desk research and the capture of existing data) can take place and the information it produces can be recorded.

## 5. Data analysis

This is the "number-crunching" element of research, most often involving computer analysis. The captured data need to be sorted – for example, tables produced showing the total response and that of individual groups within the total. Precision is necessary here and at the end an accurate picture must be able to be set out.

## 6. Reporting

Any research project of any size is likely to result in a written report. In addition, this is usually summarized by an agency in a formal presentation. The report of the research must:

» present the findings clearly, concisely, and in a way that links specifically to the original brief; and
» draw conclusions and suggest action, or at least begin to do so (some agencies are hardly involved in this stage, just presenting the facts – indeed that may be what a client wants – others make a virtue of seeing the analysis through).

Whoever does what at this stage, it is the final analysis and consideration of conclusions and an action-oriented conclusion to the project that gives it its real value. Whether the action is low-key or high-profile, it is this that makes research worthwhile.

While projects vary in nature and scale, this broad approach would be descriptive of many and certainly gives an idea of the process involved.

## MAKING IT WORK

Next we look in this section at a series of examples and experiences that, together, are included to exemplify the research process. Only sensible research is likely to assist marketing. The fact that it is a form of investigation does not mean every answer or result is going to be invaluable, especially if there is a fault in the method or rationale. For example, the following was not the finest hour of those involved:

» CPC International, producers of the Knorr brand, conducted taste tests in the US which solely involved serving freshly made hot soup to potential customers. They liked it. But they subsequently did not buy it, because it came as dry powder in a packet – testers did not ask about this and it was only later they discovered a prejudice against this form of product.

Such a brief example, and I am sure there could be many more, shows how even seemingly simple errors can negate research producing useful information. But what about research that makes a difference?

Next, we examine a case which shows how directly market research, in this case focused on very specific aspects of a product, can directly influence a product and its marketing.

## CASE STUDY – BOOK JACKETS

Marketing communications are inherent at many stages of the marketing process, up to and including the point of sale. One of the most interesting examples of how promotions need to be researched is a case study, which was published in the Market Research Society *Survey* journal about crime writer Agatha Christie's books. Since the 1960s and before these titles had been regular bestsellers – a perennial part of a bookseller's stock.

Then publisher HarperCollins found sales were declining, but they were uncertain about the reasons for this decline. They commissioned a research company which carried out a mix of desk research, qualitative research, and quantitative research to understand the underlying trends in the market and specific reasons for the drop in sales. The desk research showed that the number of adults claiming to have bought a paperback in the previous twelve months had declined from 20.9 million to 19.6 million – which was around 1% a year. The market was biased towards the young, those in the higher socio-economic groups, and the better educated.

The next stage of the research was qualitative, taking place via four group discussions with current readers of Agatha Christie books and buyers of paperbacks. Groups of 15-24 year olds and 35-44 year olds were recruited. The groups were mixed in terms of sex and two of the four groups were ABC1 socio-economic grade – the other two were C2D. The purpose of the groups was to discover how they viewed crime writing in relation to other genres. Christie needed to be evaluated to assess her style with other writers. The group respondents were also shown the cover designs, which over 20 years had changed significantly. More group discussions were also carried out with "non-readers," those who had only seen Christie films or read other crime books.

The findings of the groups confirmed that there was interest in crime writing, with Christie being viewed as the "queen of crime." Christie crimes were perceived to provide "active reading," the murders in her books are always "nice," and her style invites participation. Most of the books feature her characters Hercule Poirot or Miss Marple, and it was these characters rather than the author that may deter people from buying books. With Christie books visual presentation was also found to be important. The groups found that the current book jackets did not convey the qualities of the author. They featured blood and gore, following a trend in the book market which had seen a rise in the sales of horror books. The research showed that the Christie readers turned away from the gory aspects of crime, not being interested in those details. It seemed it was the "horror style" covers that were causing the sales to decline.

HarperCollins produced a sales pack for the sales representatives to use when calling on their main customers, the bookshop chains, providing all the details of the research. In addition a sales campaign was launched and totally new packaging was created. After the campaign four more group discussions were completed to identify if readers noticed any differences. The new jacket designs were perceived as intriguing and subtle. The pictures on the jacket were seen to link with the title and the design was felt to convey quality. The new theme for the covers was developed into point-of-sale promotions and advertising.

As a result of this research, sales of Agatha Christie paperbacks increased by 40% in the first year following the change – 1 million units increasing to 1.4 million units. This case study shows the importance of checking with potential buyers before considering any changes in presentation of a product. It also shows that marketing benefits can be obtained from research very quickly after the research has been completed.

It shows that research helps to understand what consumers consider to be the "unique selling points" of a product or service. Once identified, they can be incorporated in the marketing communications and tested out by researching concepts. If USPs are targeted well then the current and potential customers will relate to them and confirm through research that they will be effective in marketing the product.

## CASE STUDY – PACKAGING MATERIALS

Sometimes the results of market research can prompt radical action. Here a complete change to marketing strategy occurred. This case involves a packaging company whose main product base was the manufacture of high quality printed cartons and boxes. The company had recently invested in the most modern production plant, capable of producing superior quality products at lower costs and with a reduced turnaround compared to their competitors. Once the plant was in operation, it was realized that the necessary production volumes were not being achieved from the sales orders to make the plant viable. So the company decided to carry out market research with its existing and potential customers to establish its market profile, before deciding how to develop a strategy to obtain an increase in market share.

In-depth interviews were carried out with the major purchasers in the market to establish their attitudes towards the leading suppliers of packaging in terms of price, delivery, quality, and general company image. Each individual supplier was rated in these terms against the other suppliers. The original packaging company had believed that the results would show their company to be amongst the leaders in quality and delivery performance, but average in terms of price.

The market research results, however, were not as expected. In fact, the results suggested that the company was bottom of the league on all factors except quality. In addition, it showed that the company had an overall image of being a slow-reacting company, only to be used for special work not required quickly and where price was not important.

These results obviously surprised the company, and they did not provide the answer to how to increase the volume throughput and the commercial viability of the production plant. However, as the results were being considered by management, certain more positive features became apparent.

First, management realized that the quality image was favorable, and that it was a major reason why the company had the image of being a specialist work supplier. Secondly, the comments on poor delivery had been those associated with the company some time back, before its investment program, and the buyers interviewed were not necessarily aware of the new plant and production facilities. Lastly, the perception of specialist work did not link with pricing, which was considered unimportant in this area.

Clearly the company's initial marketing strategy of being a high-volume, low-cost, and quality producer was at variance with the market's image. It was also apparent from the results that a more significant market niche was available. Since its image was specialist, and once the message of increased volume with rapid delivery could be passed into the market, it would be possible for the company to increase its market share. More importantly, as this type of work was not price-sensitive, higher profits could be made without direct comparison to competitive suppliers.

Here we have seen that the expected results of the market research were not obtained and the company's initial marketing approach appeared to be failing. As a result of the market research, intuitive analysis of the outcome showed that a definite marketing approach was possible, which could provide greater success than had initially been targeted in the marketing plan. The market research gave the company much more actionable results than had been thought possible in the initial marketing planning.

Now, to tie in with Chapter 3, which demonstrated that research fits easily with the process of international marketing, we look at two more cases, both from Asian markets, that demonstrate the value of research in very different product areas.

## CASE STUDY – REFRIGERATION CONTROL MARKET IN MYANMAR (BURMA)

This European company is a major manufacturer of components used in making refrigeration equipment. It is one of the top brands in this market. The Singapore office was set up in 1980 to develop the Asian market. Over the years, the office has grown in size and has more than 50 people covering all aspects of manufacturing, marketing, and servicing for the South East Asian markets. Products were selling very well in all of South East Asia except Myanmar, in which it did not sell at all, one reason being the political boycott by the EU and US because of the country's human rights record. With a population of 47 million, the market is felt to be too big to ignore.

A brief study of the Myanmar market shows that there is a significant market in the seafood industry, which is a major market segment of this European company. However, Myanmar has a very closed and undeveloped economy, and very little information was available of the industries there. The only thing that was known was that the country has 2700 kilometers of coastline with a substantial fishing industry along the coast. The manager in charge decided to visit the country to survey the market.

## Investigation

A visit showed that there was a cluster of seafood processing plants along the coast near the capital city of Yangon (Rangoon). They constituted more than half the plants in the entire country. It was felt that an understanding of the refrigeration market in these seafood plants near Yangon would be sufficient to gain an understanding of the whole market. The equipment used for the refrigeration process included freezers, ice-making machines, freezer storage, and cold rooms. The manager visited each plant around Yangon to find out how they purchased their refrigeration plants and the associated controls.

## Results

The survey showed that all the major brands of the world were used in the refrigeration controls of the seafood processing plants, including the brand of this European manufacturer. The plants had been supplied, on a turnkey basis, by three contractors based in Malaysia and Singapore. Spare parts, including the refrigeration controls, were bought from an importer who went to Singapore regularly for his purchases. The European manufacturer was able to sell to Myanmar indirectly through the three contractors in Malaysia and Singapore, thereby circumventing the political boycott of Myanmar.

There is nothing sophisticated about the method employed here. Just defining what information was needed and getting out and asking face-to-face produced good results. Research changed a market producing nothing to one producing significant business, and identified a cost-effective way of accessing it.

## CASE STUDY – TIGER BEER IN ASIA

Tiger beer is made by a brewery in Singapore, which is a joint venture between Heineken and a Singapore group of companies in the food and beverage industry. Over the past years, it has carved out a good brand image and large market share in Singapore. In the early 1990s, it decided to expand in the regional markets in Asia. A market survey was commissioned.

### Investigation

Tiger is a small player in the world market and it decided not to compete with the big boys in the established markets in Asia, where more and more international brands had appeared over recent years. Only careful desk research was necessary to ascertain the pattern of the market around the region. Sales were identified for the big players, which included Budweiser, Miller, Heineken, Carlsberg, Beck's, etc. At the same time, further research showed the strong position of local brands in certain parts of the region. It decided not to consider several Asian markets where there were very strong local brands. These included Japan (Kirin, Asahi and Sapporo), Korea (OB), Thailand (Singha), Philippines (San Miguel), and Indonesia (Anker).

### Results

The above survey needed only to examine the quantitative picture of existing brands across the various markets in the region to show that there were niche areas where Tiger had the opportunity of establishing itself as a key player in the market. These included Vietnam, Myanmar, Kampuchea, and less developed parts of China. Immediate action was able to create the basis of successful business in these areas which, given the strong quality image of Tiger beer, can be used to build successful ongoing business.

In due course, with wider distribution and franchise Tiger may well be able to take further steps to lift its business outside its home market. Maybe more research will help with this at a later date.

Both these cases show the value of having clear information as a basis for decision-making. The research itself was simple enough in the sense that it was not necessary to interview people in their hundreds or thousands – the facts discovered led directly to good decision-making, and to successful business growth based on the rapid exploitation of opportunities found to exist.

To complete this section and fill out the picture still further we examine one last case.

## CASE STUDY – USING RESULTS TO INFLUENCE THE MARKET SUCCESSFULLY

The final case concerns a company supplying artificial flavorings to major food producers. It had as its main competitor a company marketing "natural flavorings." In reality, both products were derived from natural raw materials. The larger company reprocessed the product to allow ease of use and greater consistency for its customers' processes. As a result it had the major part of the market. However, the competitor tried to emphasize its products' "natural state," despite the fact that productivity gains obtained from the processed product were advantageous to the user, and no apparent difference could be detected in the final end product so far as the producer was concerned.

The lead company's American counterpart was experiencing major marketing problems with a similar situation in its home market. Again, there was an alternative "natural product" produced by a company who successfully used this "natural" profile. As a result of exchange rate changes, the prospect of this American product being available at a competitive price in the UK, marketed according to this natural profile, became a possibility.

The UK lead company, recognizing the impending competition from the US product and the possible resurgence of its domestic competition, questioned how this would affect their market. It therefore briefed a market research consultancy to analyze the situation and recommend what activities should be undertaken to protect its markets. It became clear that no one knew what the real effect of the flavoring was on the product, beyond its normal technical use. The research consultancy suggested a program of market research to examine any differences perceived, not by the manufacturer, but by the users and consumers about the three flavorings within the product.

Conventional consumer quantitative research through hall testing was carried out with all three products. The expected outcome of the research was that consumers would perceive no difference and that "naturalness" would not be an issue. In fact, the research, although confirming this latter issue, did not give an even result between the variants, but suggested that consumers felt that the end product with the lead company's flavoring gave an added quality to the product.

The lead company was now in a very strong position to action these results in an aggressive marketing campaign, designed to show its customers that their consumers could differentiate between flavorings and that its product was preferred. The outcome of the research gave a leading edge to the UK company and this was subsequently marketed very efficiently to its benefit.

It is also worth commenting that, had the market research findings been negative to the UK company, it would nevertheless have been ready to establish a technical research and development program to overcome any product deficiencies and create a difference. Clearly, the market research was the linchpin of the company's decision-making process and the results led to successful marketing activity.

In this situation, the company had recognized a marketing problem, had explored the extent of the problem through market research and, when the results were obtained, used them to influence its market significantly.

While sometimes the results of research are unspectacular, on occasion – as here – they both surprise *and* provide significant opportunity.

## SUMMARY

Observations show that:

» research is regularly used, and for many organizations is a basic part of their thinking and decision-making;

» good research needs care and a thorough approach to everything, from defining what it is aiming to do through to analysis and interpretation of the results; and
» though no panacea, research can provide real opportunity to improve marketing effectiveness and reduce risk.

# Key Concepts and Thinkers

"The key to using information efficiently lies in the ability to define exactly what information is required. This is a valuable management skill. Defining the problem or defining the research objectives is the first step in the market research process."

*P.R. Smith, author "Marketing Communications - an integrated approach"*

This is a technical business and there is plenty of jargon, as ever with a specialist business technique, so we start with a glossary: everything a manager must know to use and perform with research effectively - and be seen to be "in the know" about it. Well, maybe not everything; the list of technical terms that could be included here would take over this work.

## GLOSSARY

**Attitude statements** - A psychological concept designed to evaluate and investigate values, beliefs, and motives for different forms of behavior.

Developing statements to describe your company and its products and services compared with those of your competitors provides the means of creating a "control," measuring consumer opinion as to whether they agree or disagree with the attitudes, and, in time, monitoring the changes.

**Attribute** - Factors identifying differences between people such as age, sex, or location (also applied to differences between brands).

**Bayesian statistics** - Combining previously estimated probabilities with survey-derived information to assist decision-making.

**Blind testing** - Research where opinion is canvassed, for example about a product - a specific brand - without revealing the brand identity. Thus in hall tests, for example, product packaging would be disguised.

**Box-Jenkins** - A method of statistical forecasting which is based on time series.

**Classification** - The questions asked in a questionnaire that define the respondent, i.e. the person's age, marital status, whether they are a home owner, etc.

**Cluster analysis** – A technique of multivariate analysis, which identifies groups of individuals that are similar to and different from each other. It is a way of establishing whether a group of people have similar attitudes or characteristics, which helps to define or confirm sub-segments of a market.

It is an important technique for defining which types of product suit different types of consumer and also for establishing whether communications can be developed for specific market segments.

**Coding** – The process of making a questionnaire able to be analyzed (usually by computer), especially to make analysis of open-ended questions that express opinion easier.

**Concept testing** – This is research designed to gain an idea of consumers' reactions to something new. It might be applied to many things – a potential new product, a new advertisement – and is carried out *before* finalizing, say, production arrangements.

**Conjoint analysis** – A method of evaluating consumer preferences among product concepts, which vary in respect of several attributes, based on asking people to rank which they most and least prefer.

Using this analysis helps to develop data on how certain types of customer have a preference for purchasing and using certain types of product. It will therefore define what is the ideal product for customers by establishing how well the product meets their needs.

**Consumer panel** – A selected sample of individuals used to track trends, with their behavior being recorded over a period of time.

**Delphi method** – A method of prediction that statistically derives a consensus view from a group of experts.

**Demographics** – Sex, age, and social grade are the key parts of the classification data in research and comprise the demographics of the market being researched.

It is vital for defining a market initially to know who are the current and potential customers. It has to become the basic "benchmark" data on which psychographic analyses are developed and created.

**Depth interview** – An interview which, rather than prompting a respondent to complete prescribed questions, takes a directed, but more free-form approach, and is in a form that is more conversational than question/answer.

**Desk research** - This is based on the use of secondary data, collecting all published and existing information that is relevant to the company's markets and products. Collection of this information is important in understanding markets and helping to design surveys, ensuring that a survey does not collect data that already exists.

**Exponential smoothing** - Another statistical technique, this uses a weighting approach and smoothes time series and helps prepare short-term projections.

**Family life cycles** - Stages in the development of families–young single people and young couples, the early stage; couples with children at home, the mid-life stage; and older people without children, the late stage.

**Field force** - The people forming the team, from a research department or agency, which actually carries out the job of obtaining information (by whatever means - interviewing, etc). Many are freelance and gathered together project by project. What they do is usually referred to as **field work**.

**Forecasting** - Estimating the expected quantity of probability of an event in the future. It may also be a prediction mode using a mathematical model, or from an extrapolation of current trends.

This is important as a technique in a defined market, which can be tracked by monitoring key facts, habits, and activities of the market which has been classified. It is particularly useful as a way of analyzing products and product performances if product design or formulation is changed to alter the market or sales in the market.

**Geodemographics** - A method of classifying households based on multivariate analysis of data from the census of population. The practical application of geodemographic classifications generally depends on computer-matching addresses to enumerate districts by means of the postcode (or zip code).

The application of geodemographics is useful for direct marketing, retail planning, or developing promotions and specific marketing activities for monitoring markets or ethnic groups.

**Hall test** - A test requiring physical exposure to the product (e.g. tasting a food product), where respondents are gathered in a central location, often a public hall of some sort - hence the name.

**Image statements** – Consumers' perceptions or impressions of your company, product, or service expressed in a clear statement.

These are used to establish how close to, or far away from, consumer needs, your ideas, concepts, and strategies are.

**In-house research** – Research conducted directly by the organization seeking the information, rather than sub-contracted to a specialist market research agency of some sort.

**Likert scale** – A scale used to rate levels and types of opinion by asking people to express their level of agreement or disagreement with a statement of some sort. Also known simply as an agree/disagree scale, many people are familiar with this from surveys they complete.

**Market mapping** – A "map" which shows the relative positions of the products in the market, consumers, or consumer characteristics. It is the most effective method for summarizing the findings of attitude research.

There are two applications for market mapping. The first is literally to draw up the structure of the market and to add to the map the facts about each level of the market – the volume of sales, the classification of the customer types, etc. It is particularly good for understanding a market more clearly.

The second is to use the analysis of survey research and to plot on a map the relationship between the defined customer types and the way in which attitudes are described or product attributes are rated. It is good for developing a product or communications strategy in sophisticated markets where it is important to develop strategies to respond to consumers' changing and demanding needs to counter competitive threats.

**Market segmentation** – Using classifications or market facts to divide a market into the characteristics of the product or service, user, and buyer in the market, type, or size of company.

A central and very important marketing technique, market segmentation is a key tool to making research useful to grow business. It allows customer types and their different needs to be analyzed, interpreted, and monitored effectively. It assists in understanding how the market divides and how customers behave in different ways with different needs.

**Marketing information system** – All the information available to management, together with the hardware for its storage, processing, and retrieval. Market intelligence, reports from all departments, and market research are all part of this system.

Creating, using, and monitoring such a system is important for making the organization customer-oriented.

**Modeling** – A model is a summary of observations, including mathematical models. It is a way of "imitating" or "copying" the market forces and testing out changes in a market and then observing the effects that result.

It is a technique which is particularly effective in product and service research. It helps to anticipate market changes and move quickly once the effects of competitors' activity are re-analyzed in the model.

**Motivational research** – Research that attempts to ascertain not just first-level opinion (do you like this or not?) but also *why* people act as they do.

**Multivariate techniques** – Multivariate techniques are those which examine the relationships among a number of variables. They include analysis of variance, multi-regression, factor and principal component analysis, cluster analysis, and discriminant analysis.

Application of these techniques to survey analysis provides the manager with the opportunity to advance product and communications planning. It helps to translate the methods of marketing into the language and behavior of consumers.

**Numerical scale** – Another classic way of measuring opinion – to simplify, it asks for a view "on the scale where, say, 10 is excellent and 1 is unsatisfactory" or the like.

**Paired comparison test** – A test to compare two products or samples with the purpose of getting a user or buyer to discriminate between them or identify changes or improvements.

It is an important way of developing data to identify users' and buyers' attitudes to competitors' products and establish consumers' perceived benefits of your own.

**Placement test** – Research that does more than just show people something an opinion is required about, but allows them to test it for a period in their office or home.

**Psychographic analysis** – A segmentation application that classifies people into groups based on their behavior or attitudes.

It is becoming more and more important as a technique as it helps to classify and group the customers in a market, reflecting their needs in the context of their preferences and buying habits. It helps to make communications more direct and relevant and to make market analysis more realistic in the context of getting to know the customer.

**Qualitative research** – Research that does not attempt to make measurements, but which seeks insights through less structured and more flexible approaches.

**Quantitative research** – This, unlike qualitative research, seeks to make specific measurements (for example, assessing market size or share).

**Regression analysis** – A statistical method of calculating an equation which is applied to a set of bivariate or multivariate observations.

It is a useful technique for analyzing different market segments to identify whether any of the sub-groups of customer have any similarities in behavior, attitudes, or preferences.

**Sample** – A segment which is representative of the whole, whose purpose is to be able to investigate the characteristics of the population. It is comprised of parts or sub-sets of the population being researched. Survey research depends on getting this right, as a survey completed with the wrong type of population is worthless. The statistics of this are a whole separate area of study.

**Sampling** – The technique for selecting a sample. It depends on setting up a sampling frame and identifying sampling units, which comprise a population.

Survey research is only successful if this is completed well.

**Syndicated research** – This is research conducted by, or on behalf of, a group of collaborators (for example, several companies in one industry) where the costs and the results are shared. It reduces costs and results in valuable research being conducted that would otherwise be ruled out on grounds of cost.

**Time series** – A set of sequential values taken over a period of time.

**Tracking survey** – A survey that gathers information to create not simply a picture of how things are now, but how they change over a period of time. It is concerned with the trends as much as the facts, and results need showing graphically to ensure effective interpretation.

**Trade-off models** – A technique which is used to discover the most attractive combination of attributes for a product or service by the respondent expressing a preference for one or other alternative.

An important technique for understanding clearly the reasons *why* people buy and how they evaluate whether the product or service that is offered corresponds with their needs and the way in which they decide on making the purchase.

**Weighting** – A process that assigns numerical coefficients to each of a series of elements, this is done to provide them with the appropriate degree of importance relative one to another. Weighted samples and other expressions relate to this methodology.

**NOTE**: This glossary is drawn in part from *The Dictionary of Market Research*, published by the Market Research Society. Though space prohibits us from adding to the list of entries here, reference is made to the other, more comprehensive, glossaries mentioned in Chapter 9.

## KEY CONCEPTS AND THINKERS

Market research crops up as a component part of the writing of all the well-known marketing gurus and, though they do not spend long on it within the context of the marketing process overall, some comment is useful. Philip Kotler (whose *Marketing Management* textbook has not a dozen pages on it, amongst more than 800) has a useful overview of the characteristics of good market research, which are paraphrased below.

» *The use of an essentially scientific method*: that is, careful observation, formulation of a possible hypothesis, prediction, and then testing to arrive at conclusions.
» *Research creativity*: a constant search for innovative methods of solving problems rather than sticking with the status quo.
» *Using multiple methods*: a shying away from reliance on one single method, a recognition that multiple methods lead to better information and a willingness to adapt the method to the task, rather than the other way round.

» *Interdependence of models and data*: a recognition that data are interpreted from underlying models which guide the type of information required.

» *Value and cost of information*: a balancing of the value of information against cost.

» *A healthy skepticism*: not assuming that the nature of the market is known either by the researchers or the managers commissioning it.

» *Ethical marketing practice*: the belief that research should benefit both the organization doing it and the customers of that organization also.

This ties in well with other ways of viewing the market research process, and, as usual with Kotler, gets to the key issues succinctly.

## THE FATHER OF MARKET RESEARCH

The name that comes first to mind in thinking about market research is that of George Gallup. Born in 1901 in Iowa, his psychology PhD was titled *An Objective Method for Determining Reader Interest in the Content of a Newspaper* and began the use of scientifically selected samples. In the early 1930s, a published article prompted Raymond Rubicam to approach him and move him to New York. In Young and Rubicam he ran the first political poll (correctly predicting the election of his mother-in-law), and set in train the many polls now conducted to test the opinion of wide populations.

In the UK, Mark Abrams might be considered to qualify for the same description. He invented social research and made a major contribution to technique development; more so than Gallup in the past.

The complexity of market research is considerable; certainly to the extent that there are a large number of elements and processes, all of which must be orchestrated together to make effective market research a reality. Some are themselves essentially specialist, for example, those matters linked to statistical methodology.

## GETTING A HANDLE ON RESPONDENTS

It is a necessity for research that people are categorized into homogenous groups. When those researched are already a tightly defined group (arable farmers with more than 1000 acres in Hertfordshire and Essex, or whatever) there is little problem. In researching products that sell to the population at large, there is. Various systems are used to classify people into socio-economic groups. As an example, the main system currently used in the UK is shown in the box below.

## CURRENTLY USED SOCIO-ECONOMIC CLASSES (BASED ON THE OCCUPATION OF THE HEAD OF A FAMILY UNIT)

» **Class 1a**: Large employers, higher manager. Company director. Senior police/fire/prison/military officer. Newspaper editor. Football manager (with squad of 25 plus). Restaurateur.
» **Class 1b**: Professionals. Doctor. Solicitor. Engineer. Teacher. Airline pilot.
» **Class 2**: Associate professionals. Journalist. Nurse/midwife. Actor/musician. Military NCO. Junior police/fire/prison officer. Lower managers (fewer than 25 staff).
» **Class 3**: Intermediate occupations. Secretary. Air stewardess. Driving instructor. Footballer (employee sportsman). Telephone operator.
» **Class 4**: Small employees/managers, non-professional self-employed. Publican. Plumber. Golfer/tennis player (self-employed sportsman). Farm owner/manager (fewer than 25 employees).
» **Class 5**: Lower supervisors, craft and related workers. Electrician. Mechanic. Train driver. Building site/factory foreman. Bus inspector.
» **Class 6**: Semi-routine occupations. Traffic warden. Caretaker. Gardener. Supermarket shelf stacker. Assembly line worker.
» **Class 7**: Routine occupation. Cleaner. Waiter/waitress/bar staff/ messenger/courier. Road-worker. Docker.
» **Class 8**: Excluded. Long-term unemployed. Never worked. Long-term sick.

## CORE TECHNIQUES

Given the complexity of the market research process, there are concepts and techniques aplenty, many are touched on in the glossary and in various ways throughout this work. Two deserve special mention because they are key to the whole process, and it seems appropriate to spend some time on them here. The first relates to getting in the data on which market research operates.

## 1. Questionnaire design

Sounds easy, but collecting information – asking the right questions – needs care and precision; without this, the information collected may be limited or worthless. Often, in fact, criticisms of research are based on poor research that is ineffective in this specific area.

Questionnaire design has to produce a document that is:

» easy to administer, read out, or fill in by both an interviewer and an informant;
» constructed in a way that answers the research hypothesis or research problem, but also has the capability to identify new issues;
» easy to analyze and can provide all the characteristics of the informant being interviewed; and
» constructed recognizing both what is known already and the new data it is designed to collect.

The key point to remember about questionnaire design is to make the interview possible for all those using the document. It has to have the following characteristics.

» *A logical sequence*: This is important, as the questions must follow on logically one from another. If they do, the interviewer will establish and maintain a rapport and collect the data required without interruptions caused by the respondent being uncertain, or repetitive questions. Intrusive questions are more likely to be answered if they are inserted into the sequence once the rapport has been established and built.
» *Good wording*: The successful questions – those questions that ensure that a survey is successful – are those that are short, specific, clear, and unambiguous. They help the informant by specifying clearly what you want to evaluate and where possible show examples or illustrations with detailed descriptions.
» *Write a clear layout*: A questionnaire is a working document. A question, the possible list of answers precoded on the questionnaire,

the instructions to the interviewers, and the analysis instructions all have to be clear so that the interviewer does not get confused or read out the wrong words. Distinguish between all of these very carefully. Interviewers' instructions should be in capitals and underlined. Hand-out cards and visual prompts should be large enough to be read, even by informants with poor sight. If the next question to be asked depends on the answer to the current question, routing and "slip" instructions should be printed alongside the relevant answers clearly to help the logical sequence.

» *A reasonable length*: A street or doorstep interview should not last more than 10 minutes. An in-home interview should be no more than 30 minutes to one hour. A shop or trade interview or business-to-business interview should not last more than 45 minutes. And often reality means people will give up less time than this.

A questionnaire which is of reasonable length means one which is sufficiently long to collect the required information. It is ideally one that is interesting to the informant and it should be able to help the informant to learn about their attitude to the subject or issue being researched.

Good questions depend on good design, but this can vary when behavior and attitudes have to be measured and monitored. The essential part of monitoring behavior is to obtain an accurate recall of what a person did. The effective way of doing this is to ask a series of questions about recent events that the informant might relate to – *when did you last look at, buy, or talk to . . .?*

Attitudes, opinions, and images are generally measured by developing scales. Verbal scales are more easily understood than numerical scales or making a rating which takes a score out of ten. There are also different options for scales:

» *unipolar scales*: a five-point scale from "Good" to "Not Very Good";
» *bipolar scales*: a five-point scale from "Very Good" to "Very Bad";
» *rating scales based on getting some type of agreement to statements*: "Agree Strongly, Agree, Neither Agree nor Disagree, Disagree, and Disagree Strongly" provides this analysis; and
» *smiley scales*: are used for children.

Finally, all questionnaires must collect classification data. These are needed to finish the interview effectively. There are essentially three reasons for this:

» to ensure the right person is collected for the sample being researched;
» to validate the interview in quality control procedures as laid down in the Codes of Conduct of the survey research sector (and the data protection legislation); and
» to collect factors which can be used as variables for analysis.

What is increasingly important about classification data is that they must be used to develop more information on the habits and lifestyle of the informants. This is used to analyze and explain the answers given to the rest of the questionnaire.

A good questionnaire is one that examines the habits, awareness, attitudes, and needs of an informant and how all of these relate. In this way consumer behavior can be analyzed, understood, and even simulated to predict how it could change. Questionnaire design is an art and not a science, and therefore it depends on an individual's creative powers to get it right.

## 2. Computer analyses

Data analysis has an important function in making information not just actionable but effective for developing conclusions and recommendations from the research. The analysis may assist the data user to interpret and understand aspects of the data that may not have originally been realized. In fact, poor data analysis may cause the research to appear to be useless, and so each data set that is developed has to be checked carefully.

The basic analysis technique, as in Table 8.1, is to look at the results of each question, analyzed by the classification data – age, sex, and social class, type of company, number of employees, and turnover. This provides the initial "picture in the frame of the movie" and quickly indicates which aspect of the information is interesting, which is useful, and which can be interpreted for further implications. Often, when the interpretation is made, it is realized that further analysis is required. One question might have to be cross-analyzed with another question to identify the strength of opinion of one of the key groups that have been classified. Key groups may need to be regrouped into different classifications to look at the significance of the results within the original groups, as the initial classification may have been too general (Table 8.2 illustrates).

**Table 8.1** Example of a basic question analysis.
Q1: Do you know the answer to this question?
Base: All who were asked the question.

|  | Total | Age | | | Region | |
|---|---|---|---|---|---|---|
|  |  | 18–34 | 35–44 | 45–65 | North | South |
| Total | 300 | 100 | 150 | 5 | 98 | 202 |
|  | 100% | 100% | 100% | 100% | 100% | 100% |
| Yes | 266 | 92 | 142 | 42 | 85 | 181 |
|  | 83% | 92% | 95% | 84% | 86% | 90% |
| No | 24 | 8 | 8 | 8 | 12 | 12 |
|  | 12% | 8% | 5% | 16% | 12% | 6% |
| Refused | 10 | – | – | – | 1 | 9 |
|  | 5% |  |  |  | 1% | 9% |

Some surveys also indicate attitude statements that require statistical measures in the tables. Usually the respondents in the survey have been asked to say how much they agree or disagree with a particular statement. The computer allocates a score to the answers, +2 for Agree Strongly to −2 for Disagree Strongly. Multiplying the number of respondents by each score enables the software to give the following measures:

» a mean score – an average within the sub-groups;
» a standard deviation – a measure of the average deviation of the sample from the mean; and
» a standard error of the mean – an estimate of the standard deviation of the populations from which a sample is drawn.

The most important factor in setting computer analyses is to think about the analysis you will need before designing the questionnaire.

**Table 8.2**  Example of an analysis with statistics.

|  | Total | Male | Female |
| --- | --- | --- | --- |
| Total | 1300 | 649 | 651 |
| Agree strongly (+2) | 128 | 66 | 62 |
|  | 10% | 10% | 10% |
| Agree (+1) | 535 | 283 | 252 |
|  | 41% | 44% | 39% |
| Neither agree nor disagree (0) | 312 | 136 | 176 |
|  | 24% | 21% | 27% |
| Disagree (−1) | 98 | 45 | 53 |
|  | 8% | 7% | 8% |
| Disagree strongly (−2) | 14 | 3 | 11 |
|  | 1% | – | 2% |
| Don't know | 213 | 116 | 97 |
|  | 16% | 18% | 15% |
| Mean score | 0.51 | 0.68 | 0.54 |
| STD DEV | 0.86 | 0.82 | 0.88 |
| STD ERR | 0.03 | 0.04 | 0.04 |

But sometimes this does not work out. I (RB) completed a survey a few years ago interviewing book buyers in bookshops that did not work out when we ran the computer analysis. 1000 people had been interviewed. 600 of them had been book buyers and 400 had been non-buyers, who had just visited the store. The computer analysis provided data that was divided into too many small groups to make it able to provide good data. The solution to the problem was to get someone to read all of the 1000 questionnaires and draw up an analysis of how the questionnaires had been answered, and note where certain "language" indicated the type of behavior and attitude of the informant that affected the buying pattern. The analysis of this was computed and there was a clear distinction in the interpretation of the data analysis between the different socio-economic groups in the survey.

Where computer tabulations become more complex is in the process of turning data into information, supplemented by additional analysis tools. Statistical techniques exist which, using computers, examine many variables simultaneously. This is helpful for examining interrelationships within the original data analyzed on a basic computer tabulation. These are the techniques for multivariate analysis. They are used for market segmentation, preference analysis, forecasting, and product definition.

The two types of analysis used to segment markets are factor analysis and cluster analysis. *Factor analysis* examines the responses to a battery of attitude statements. It groups those questions that have been answered in a similar way. The resultant factors are then analyzed by a *cluster analysis* that groups the respondents who answer particular questions in the same way.

The techniques for preference analysis depend on the requirements of the researcher. "Round Robin" analysis can be used to indicate if there are differences between preference ratings if the informant has rated a number of products. Conjoint analysis is used to identify whether package style is more important than the size and which is preferred.

Forecasting techniques include multiple regression and time series analysis. Product mapping is achieved by correspondence analysis and multi-dimensional scaling. Correspondence analysis is a technique that produces maps which can be easily interpreted and show which products are preferred in a similar manner.

A manager whose work might benefit from using research may well need to know what particular technique is required and when to apply it. They will not need to understand complex programming aspects of the computer analysis as they will be more interested in the results of using it. What is important is to know what analysis is required when planning the survey, and that those involved in the detail can utilize it and make it work.

After investigating two core concepts that make the research process work, let us end by considering a fundamental aspect that underlies the whole business.

## MARKETING STRATEGY

It is worth ending this section with a word about marketing strategy. Market research is, after all, only a means to an end. Its purpose is to explore and produce data that, in turn, provides information useful as one of the raw materials of decision-making. As such, its rationale is in the competitive nature of markets. Research is done ultimately for one reason alone – *to gain competitive advantage*.

Thus those wanting to study or use market research need to be familiar with the processes of setting and implementing marketing strategies. It is the market situation – and intentions for market activity – that make research generally, and particular kinds of research also, useful. As the cases in Chapter 7 clearly showed, research at its best directly impacts marketing activity and results coming from the market.

Thus readers of this section may want to explore other volumes in the ExpressExec series that look at marketing and marketing strategy in particular (series numbers 04.01–04.10).

# Resources

- » Useful organizations
- » Other bodies
- » Training films
- » Magazines
- » Desk research
- » Books
- » Final word

"To carry out marketing analysis, planning implementation and control managers need information."
                    *Philip Kotler, marketing consultant and author*

Whether you need to know more about the use of market research, or are a researcher wanting to refine and add to the research techniques that you use, you will find that market research is a very well-documented area.

## USEFUL ORGANIZATIONS

Market research is a sufficiently important area, however, to have its own bodies.

### The Market Research Society

This is a professional body in the sense that members must have appropriate qualifications. It is a source of information, an overseer of standards and practice, and an educational body. Specifically, it has:

» a monthly magazine, *Research*, a quarterly journal, *The International Journal of Market Research*, and a newsletter, *MRScene* (created by one of us: RJB); and
» a Code of Practice: this is a self-regulatory code designed to maintain professional standards. Not least, it is designed to create and maintain confidence amongst those who are at the receiving end of research, i.e. if you are approached to complete a questionnaire you can be reassured if you are told it is being conducted in accordance with the code. It addresses such issues as confidentiality, the responsibilities of researchers, and special factors such as the interviewing of children. It is updated regularly and links to current issues such as the Data Protection Act. It is highly regarded within the industry and, although essentially voluntary, does have real "teeth" and successfully influences practice.

MRS can be contacted at 15 Northburgh Street, London EC1V 0JR; tel: +44 (0)20 7490 4911; fax: +44 (0)20 7490 0608, and has a Website: http://www.mrs.org.uk.
    There are similar bodies in many different countries.

## The British Market Research Association

While individuals (in agencies or in corporate bodies) belong to the MRS, above, this is the trade association of market research companies. BMRA, Devonshire House, 60 Goswell Road, London EC1M 7AD; tel: +44 (0)20 7566 3636; fax: +44 (0)20 7689 6220; e-mail: admin@bmra.org.uk; Web: http://www.bmra.org.uk.

Both the MRS and the BMRA link with others in various ways in the European Federation of Market Research Organizations. EFAMRO is incorporated in the Netherlands. The secretariat address is 167 Chiltern Court, Baker Street, London NW1 5SW. tel/fax: +44 (0)20 7486 7243; Web: http://www.efamro.org.

As an integral part of the marketing process, market research is an area to which both marketing books and magazines give some attention. So too do marketing organizations such as the Chartered Institute of Marketing, Moor Hall, Cookham, Maidenhead, Berkshire SL6 9QH; tel: +44 (0)1628 427500; fax: +44 (0)1628 427499; Web: http://www.cim.co.uk/. Also, the American Marketing Association, 311 South Wacker Drive, Suite 5800, Chicago, IL 60606, USA; tel: 001 312 542 9000; fax: 542 9001; Web: http://www.ama.org/.

## OTHER BODIES

The following may also be useful.

» American Statistical Association, 1429 Duke St., Alexandria, VA 22314-3415, USA; voice: 703-684-1221; toll-free: 888-231-3473; fax: 703-684-2037; Web: http://www.amstat.org/.
» Royal Statistical Society, 12 Errol Street, London EC1Y 8LX; tel: 020 7638 8998; fax +44 (0)20 7256 7598; Web: http://www.rss.org.uk/.
» Association of Users of Research Agencies c/o ISBA, 44 Hertford Street, London W1Y 8AE.

## TRAINING FILMS

With many topics, a quick way to get an informed overview of what is involved is to look at one of the often many training films on the subject (several films are mentioned in Chapter 9 of my *Express Exec* title on *Negotiation*, for instance). With market research, however, it is a topic on which very few films exist. Just one does the job required and is worth mentioning. This is a film made by Executive Business Channel for the BBC/Open University. *Market Analysis* gives both a clear overview of what is involved and also charts an agency-run market research project in the form of a case study to exemplify the process.

## MAGAZINES

The following are the main magazines dealing with market research and related issues; in addition, it is, of course, a topic that crops up in more general marketing and business journals.

» *ADMAP*, WARC, Farm Road, Henley-on-Thames, Oxon RG9 1EJ; tel: +44 (0)1491 411 000.
» *Journal of Advertising Research* PO. Box 25, Congers, NY 10920–0025; Web: http://www.arfsite.org/Webpages/JAR_pages/jar-home.htm.
» *Journal of Targeting, Measurement and Analysis in Marketing*, Henry Stewart Publications, Museum House, 25 Museum Street, London WC1A 1JT; tel: +44 (0)20 7323 2916; fax: +44 (0)20 7323 2918; Web: http://www.henrystewart.com/journals/jt/.
» *International Journal of Research in Marketing*, Elsevier Science, Regional Sales Office, Customer Support Department, PO Box 211, 1000 AE Amsterdam, Netherlands; tel: (+31) 20 485 3757; fax: (+31) 20 485 3432; Web: http://www.elsevier.nl/locate/ijresmar.
» *Journal of Marketing Research*: see details for American Marketing Association; Web: http://www.ama.org/pubs/jmr/.
» *Journal of Consumer Research*, The University of Chicago Press, Journals Division, PO Box 37005, Chicago, IL 60637; tel: (773) 753-3347; fax: (773) 753-0811; Web: http://www.journals.uchicago.edu/JCR/home.html.
» *Journal of Applied Statistics*, Taylor & Francis Group, 11 New Fetter Lane, London EC4P 4EE; Web: http://www.tandf.co.uk/journals/frameloader.html?http://www.tandf.co.uk/journals/carfax/02664763.html.
» *The Statistician*, Blackwell Publishers Journals, PO Box 805, 108 Cowley Road, Oxford OX4 1FH; tel: +44 (0)1865 244083; fax: +44

(0)1865 381381; Web: http://www.blackwellpublishers.co.uk/journals/RSSD/descript.htm.

## DESK RESEARCH

Bodies like the Central Statistical Office (and, more particularly, its Business Statistics Office operation) and individual commercial organizations in profusion may help identify existing data. Some organizations have undertaken published research for many years and are thus a prime source of published material. A good example is: Economist Intelligence Unit, London office – 15 Regent Street, London SW1Y 4LR, United Kingdom; tel: +44 (0)20 7830 1007; fax: +44 (0)20 7830 1023; Web: http://www.eiu.com.

In addition, there are certain other bodies associated with the activity of research to be noted. These include the following.

» Audit Bureau of Circulation (which validates circulation claims made in research conducted for or on behalf of newspapers and magazines), Saxon House, 211 High Street, Berkhamsted, Hertfordshire HP4 1AD; tel: +44 (0)1442 870800; fax: +44 (0)1442 200700; e-mail: abcpost@abc.org.uk.
» Broadcasters' Audience Research Board (having a similar role to ABC (above) with regard to television), Broadcasters' Audience Research Board Ltd, 18 Dering Street, London W1R 9AF.
» Interviewer Quality Control Scheme (an independent body verifying the quality of fieldwork); Web: http://www.bsi-global.com/Search/index.xalter.
» Joint Industry Committee for National Readership Surveys (represents the Press Research Council, Incorporated Practitioners in Advertising, and Incorporated Society of British Advertisers, all of whom have interests in research matters; it controls the National Readership Survey. This in turn is the body that defines the commonly used socio-economic grades used to segment markets and consumers).
» Outdoor Site Classification and Audience Research (the wing of the Outdoor Advertising Association concerned with research), Summit House, 27 Sale Place, London W2 1YR; tel: +44 (0)20 7973 0315; fax: +44 (0)20 7973 0318; e-mail: enquiries@oaa.org.uk; Web: http://www.oaa.org.uk/leftmenu.htm.

» Association of Survey Computing (a British Computer Society special interest group, affiliated to the Market Research Society).
» British Computer Society, 1 Sanford Street, Swindon, Wiltshire SN1 1HJ, United Kingdom; Customer Support Team tel: +44 (0)1793 417424; fax: +44 (0)1793 480270; e-mail: bcshq@hq.bcs.org.uk; Web: http://www.bcs.org.uk/.

Because of the regulations and standards which relate to market research, there are a number of bodies at work; the same is true of many developed countries.

## BOOKS

The following are chosen to provide a representative selection from amongst the many books available.

» *The Dictionary of Market Research*: This contains a very comprehensive glossary; it is published by The Incorporated Society of British Advertisers and obtainable from that body (tel: +44 (0)20 7499 7502).

### AUTHOR RECOMMENDATION

Perhaps I (Patrick Forsyth) may be permitted to recommend two books linked to my co-author, Robin Birn.

» *Using Market Research to Grow Your Business*.[1] This is not a specialist guide for researchers, but a clear, informative, and practical guide for those managers wanting to make use of market research, and understand how to do so and appreciate just what it can do for them. Also recommended is *The Effective Use of Market Research*.[2]
» *The Handbook of International Market Research Techniques*, edited by Robin Birn.[3] This is a comprehensive compendium, about 600 pages long, with chapters by a long list of experts focusing on every aspect and technique involved in the research process. If you want one major reference, this is it. This is the

first book in a series published in association with the Market Research Society.

The one classic still worth noting is *Statistical Techniques for Market Research* published in 1949, written by Robert Ferber, who was Research Professor of Economics and Business at the University of Illinois.[4] Still worth looking at today. A selection of other good books – and more modern ones – is listed below.

» Brennan, R. (1995), *Cases In Marketing Management*. Pitman Publishing, Great Britain.
» Cannon, T. (1987), *Basic Marketing – Principles and Practice*, 2nd edn, Cassell Education Limited, Great Britain. Chapter 5 – Marketing Research.
» Churchill, G.A., Jr (1995), *Marketing Research Methodological Foundations*, 6th intl edn. The Dryden Press, USA.
» Hall, D., Jones, R., & Raffo, C. (1999), *Business Studies*, 2nd edn, Causeway Press Ltd, Lancashire. Unit 37 – Marketing Research.
» Kotler, P., Armstrong, G., Saunders, J., & Wong, V. (1999), *Principles Of Marketing*, 2nd European edn, Prentice Hall Europe. Chapter 8 – Market Information and Marketing Research.
» Kumar, V. (2000), *International Marketing Research*. Prentice Hall, Upper Saddle River, NJ.
» Lamb C., Hair, J., & McDaniel C. (2001), *Essentials Of Marketing*, 2nd edn, South-Western College Publishing, Thomson Learning, USA. Chapter 6 – Segmenting and Targeting Markets, Chapter 7 – Decision Support Systems and Marketing Research.
» Postma, P. (1999), *The New Marketing Era*. McGraw-Hill, USA.
» Smith, P.R. (1998), *Marketing Communications – an integrated approach*, 2nd edn. Kogan Page, Great Britain. Chapter 5 – Understanding Markets – Market Research.

## FINAL WORD

Commenting on the importance of research in the modern world, Professor Michael J. Thomas, who is president of the Market Research Society (in 2001), said:

"The skills and inventiveness of the people working in the profession have all contributed to the past decade. In the Age of Information, these people may have found their place in the sun. We are surrounded by information, perhaps deluged by it. But is it all any good? Is it trustworthy? Is it a goldmine or a septic tank? We exist in a rapidly changing environment – the changing consumer environment; the changing business environment, more global than local; and the changing technological environment.

Many of these changes are both stimulating and for the greater good; many other changes are negative, threatening, insidious, or all three. We need to understand these changes, and data is the vehicle for recording them, analysis the means for understanding and interpreting the data."

Market research has a more important role to play in future than ever before. Any organization not checking out its potential and putting it to appropriate use may well not survive so dynamic a future.

## NOTES

1 Birn, R.J. (1984), *Using Market Research to Grow Your Business*, Pitman Publishing/Institute of Management, London.
2 Birn, R.J. (1999), *The Effective Use of Market Research*, 3rd edn. Kogan Page, London.
3 Birn, R.J. (1999), *The Handbook of International Market Research Techniques*, 2nd edn, Kogan Page, London.
4 Ferber, R, (1949), *Statistical Techniques for Market Research*. McGraw-Hill Book Company, Inc., New York.

# Ten Steps to Making
# Market Research Work

"Research is often commissioned in a hurry, with insufficient thought by marketers. Objectives may be fuzzy, action standards not established in advance, and expected use of results not spelt out beforehand."

*Hugh Davidson, consultant and author (in Even More Offensive Marketing)*

This section is not intended to exclude. Market research is a broad topic involving many different aspects and certainly many different techniques. In selecting 10 headings, the intention is to encapsulate the key issues with an emphasis on *using* market research, and to do so in a way that focuses on just how market research can help grow a business, rather than only on undertaking a market research project.

## 1. RESEARCH AS AN AID TO DECISION-MAKING

Business management inevitably involves a series of choices. Do we do this or that? Do we go in one direction or another one? Although the old style manager may have taken pride in the "feel" they had for the business and their ability to make good judgments based on little more than experience and hunch, more and more decisions in recent years are based on information. The job of market research is to provide clear, accurate information that can act to influence decisions and reduce the risk inherent in running a business. Especially important are data-influenced decisions that:

» provide a better knowledge of markets and customers;
» allow more focused decisions to be made that are based on the realities of the market and all that goes on there; or
» link to improved service and satisfaction for customers – on which all commercial success ultimately depends.

Thus the first point here stresses the link between information, the research that finds it, and the decisions that management can then make. Any organization should resist the temptation to make decisions without the benefit of information that could cost-effectively be obtained (or is already available and simply needs teasing out). The basis for making research cost-effective is largely the sensitive identification of the information required, and the omission of information that is not strictly necessary to the decision-making process. Sometimes the right information is required on an ongoing basis (see the comments about trends in "6. Tracking trends" below).

If research is done, not as a matter of course or simply because *it would be good to know*, but is led by the need to know certain things in order to be able to make specific decisions, then it should be relevant and useful. Research by the yard, as it were, is not to be recommended.

What is recommended is regular research. That way snapshots can be developed into a review of the market or situation – put together, these snapshots are like a movie, with a succession of frames creating a total picture.

## 2. RESEARCH MUST UTILIZE THE NECESSARY INFORMATION

Research is an inherent part of a marketing information system and injects a flow of data and information into an organization. This may come from ongoing evaluation or from one-off surveys and may produce either quantitative or qualitative information; or more likely both. The marketing information system must decide where information comes from (maybe from sales and financial systems as well as external measurement), what volume of information is needed (and how it will be coped with), and what frequency of information is necessary (weekly, annually, whatever). For a large organization, setting up a marketing information system on a comprehensive basis is a significant undertaking. It must be well-defined and organized and backed by sufficient resources of all sorts; for instance, people and money. Commitment and good communications are necessary if things are going to work well; a good information culture is necessary.

In addition, the way all this is viewed should be tailored to the organization so that it fits well with the overall marketing objectives and strategy. The interrelationship and co-ordination here is important, because it is, not least, in matters to do with marketing planning that the information is required.

## 3. A SOUND STATISTICAL BASIS

This heading deserves a place here but not a lengthy comment. Suffice to say that statistics play a vital and considerable role in market research and do so in two main ways.

» First, there is the question of who is asked questions. With many things – including the election polls we are all (too?) familiar with, the cost of asking everyone involved is simply prohibitive. What is needed is a *sample* – that is, a smaller group that is statistically shown to be representative of the whole group involved. This is a complex mathematical concept and this is no place to try to define at length the difference between random sample, semi-random samples, and quota samples; suffice to say, it is an essential prerequisite of much research.

» Secondly, there is a wealth of statistical techniques, from measures of dispersion to binomial distribution, used to analyze and interpret the data gathered; again, this is an inherent part of the process (even if computers do most of the work).

This is an area of considerable specialist expertise. It is certainly one that a market research agency should have. However research may be organized, it needs to be in a way that deploys suitable skills in this area.

The important point here is that statistics should be used to calculate and clarify the picture sought – not to confuse. It was a statistician who said – *there are two kinds of people in the world, those who divide the world into two kinds of people; and the rest* – statistics can be as effectively used to cloud the picture as to highlight key issues. Any research project must make sure that statistics are used appropriately; and communicated appropriately as well (see "8. The communications element" below).

## 4. ASKING THE RIGHT QUESTIONS

Whatever kind of research is going to be done, it will have at its core – questions. It may seem a simple area, but it is not, and thinking back to the last questionnaire that you completed may be enough to highlight how ambiguous questions can be. An example sticks in my mind (one of a number asked in research to demonstrate just this point). Two groups were asked the following questions.

1 *Are you in favor of smoking whilst praying?* This, perhaps not surprisingly because it does not sound the right thing to do, caused more than 90% of people to answer "No."
2 *Are you in favor of praying whilst smoking?* This, sounding better, produced 90% saying "Yes." Both questions, in fact, ask the same thing. They seek an opinion about the two activities being carried out simultaneously. Yet somehow they sound wholly different and certainly they produced radically different answers.

Just as is said of comedy – with questions, it depends how you say it. So, what is necessary is careful, better still expert, questionnaire design. Questionnaires should also be:

» clear and unambiguous;
» easy to administer, that is, in being dealt with by either someone asking the questions or someone self-completing one and hoping that it will be quick and easy;
» easy to analyze (and therefore almost certainly compatible with whatever computer system is to be used for such analysis); and
» focused on agreed issues (but perhaps, if required, capable of raising and recording matters on a wider front).

Thus questionnaires should be:

» presented in a logical sequence;
» clear in question and instruction;
» easy to complete (with a good layout and adequate space, etc.); and
» manageable in length.

Finally, questionnaires should have a sensible scale if people are going to be asked to rate things (good, bad, or horrible or whatever). There are a variety of technical methods that can be involved here (unipolar scales, smiley scales – for children, etc.). One simple point is easy to understand and thus makes a good example. That is that in simple ratings an even number of choices is usually favored (an odd number has a mid-point and, whatever the scale is called, makes the easy, unthinking response of "Average" too likely).

Everything that follows in the research process is negated if the questionnaire used is flawed in some way; great care is needed.

## 5. CHOOSING AND USING THE RIGHT TECHNIQUES

There is, as has been made clear, a wealth of techniques available to undertake research. Just what is done is one of the key decisions in any market research project. Once the objectives are clear then methodology can be considered. This is, in part, in the nature of a compromise. Research always has something of the "how long is a piece of string" to it, indeed, one thing of which to be wary is unscrupulous market researchers who over-engineer the task and create an unnecessarily large bill in the process.

So what is nearly always necessary is a mix of techniques. Take an example. An company manufacturing machinery used for food packaging sells its machines to food packagers (of, amongst other things, ready cooked meals). But its business is also dependent on the sale of the resultant products to consumers and how the shops such products are bought from operate. So research needs to look at the needs of the packaging companies, the requirements of supermarkets and other retailers, and perhaps also the feelings of the ultimate consumers about ready cooked meals. Thus a research project might utilize:

» telephone interviews with food packaging companies;
» face-to-face interviews as above;
» written questionnaires sent to retail buyers;
» discussion groups of food consumers about their requirements; and
» product tests (hall tests).

With any such mix the costs dictate to some extent. Numbers must be sufficiently high to ensure statistical validity, but small numbers in some areas may also be significant. For example, in the above example, the bulk of the interviews with food packaging companies might be on the telephone, but some face-to-face will fill in detail and give a clearer picture. To have all of them face-to-face, however, might simply be prohibitively expensive. While even a small number of discussion groups could add useful information from actual food consumers at comparatively modest cost.

There is a real skill in deciding upon such a mix, making sure that it suits the research job to be done, and that it can be done in a sensible time and for a sensible budget.

## 6. TRACKING TRENDS

Necessarily much of the comment here has been about market research in the sense of a survey. Some market research is of a one-off nature; for example, two merged companies may want to check how the new joint company is now seen, and do so by conducting a perception survey. But other applications are ongoing.

A simple example is the questionnaires in a hotel. Usually placed in the bedrooms, they provide, or those completed do, regular feedback about customers' views of service standards. A careful monitoring of their comments will show not just the picture at a particular moment, but the trends – more and more people want links for their computer in their rooms or whatever it may be.

There are many applications for research where the task is logically to monitor matters on a regular basis. This might mean an annual survey of some sort, or indeed, more regular assessment. Such *tracking surveys* as they are called may be directed in many ways. Particularly, however, they may monitor marketing activity (checking the effectiveness of promotion or sales activity in some form, for instance), or gain understanding about the changing needs and expectations of buyers. Some such surveys are organized jointly, for example, several different organizations collaborating to commission *syndicated research*, the results of which will be available to all.

Ongoing research of this nature is not always necessary or appropriate. It is certainly valid to mention it here as a key issue. Regarding one-off research findings and the definitive view past their ''sell date'' is a mistake. Research findings have a finite life and some issues are so important that regular monitoring to keep views up to date makes good sense.

## 7. USING THE SPECIALISTS

Although research can be conducted by an organization acting alone (though recognizing that it demands specialist skills), much is carried out by market research agencies specializing in this sort of work for a variety of clients. These vary in type as one might suspect. Some are large, some small and, more particularly, they may specialize in a certain kind of research or in work in a particular industry. Working through an agency does not mean everything can be left to them; what the client does also affects quality.

A number of things are important.

1 Check the agency carefully, and especially for their experience in the kind of work and kind of field involved.
2 Decide how broad the involvement should be. There are various ways of operating, but a firm that is to be involved in the interpretation of the data collected might be more likely to go about its collection in the best possible way.
3 Write a clear brief. You may involve the agency in thinking this through, but you need to specify to them what needs to be done.
4 Involve everyone internally who will be using the data. It is disruptive to a project if half-way through somebody is saying "perhaps we could also put down a question about . . ." and everything has to be changed. Communication is always important throughout a project.
5 Evaluate research company proposals carefully (you should talk to more than one with relevant experience) especially in seeing how their recommendations link to their experience.
6 Confirm all details of what is ultimately agreed in writing so that there can be no misunderstanding.
7 Remember that if the brief changes on the way through – so too will costs and timing.
8 Work *with* the agency. Talk to them. Tell them everything you know and be open about what you want.

A well-judged approach as itemized here is the way to a smooth-running project that produces quality research and relevant and actionable findings that will actually help.


# 8. THE COMMUNICATIONS ELEMENT

This has been mentioned in terms of the brief to and relationship with a research firm (see "7. Using the specialists" above). Having completed some research, there may be a variety of people around an organization that need to know about it. It must not gather dust on the shelves of the marketing department, it must be widely disseminated.

This may involve the following.

1 A report. This will be prepared by the agency if one is used, but whoever writes it, it must be good. It needs to be clear. Key points must not be buried in a mass of meaningless statistics and it must make its recommendations (and the facts that influenced them) clear without too much jargon and no gobbledegook.
2 It should be graphically clear. The figures and statistics inevitably involved need to be turned into a form (bar charts, etc.) that are clear to those who have a role to play, but are laymen in research terms.
3 A presentation. This is also important in making things clear and is an important opportunity for questions to be asked. There may need to be a meeting when the research company presents, and then other, internal, meetings to pass messages on. Considering who attends all such gatherings is important.

Finally, remember that research may have implications that go well into the future. Not only do people have to be made aware of these, they may need to be reminded of them as time passes.

## 9. ANALYZING THE DATA

It is axiomatic that research does not provide ready-made answers to business problems. Nor, incidentally, does it remove the necessity for sound judgment; experience and even gut feel about markets and customers will always have their place. So it is important to regard the data collected in the right way. If the research techniques have been well chosen and are directed at asking the right questions, then the data collected are likely to be useful. But what is immediately to hand may be a seemingly unintelligible mountain of data; figures without end or meaning.

The process of analysis, most often the province of computers and computer experts if the research is on any scale, is an important bridge between simply collecting data and being able to interpret them in a way that enables it to assist good decision-making.

Questions may be asked in many forms.

» *Single choice*: What is your favorite hotel?
» *Multiple choice*: How did you make your hotel booking?
» *Numbers*: How many times have you stayed at this hotel in the last 12 months?
» *Written opinion*: How could the hotel service be improved?
» *Attitude opinion*: Do you agree/disagree with the following statements?

And they may need ascribing to a host of categories of people in terms of their characteristics: age, social class, occupation, etc. (people broken down by age and sex, as they say).

Only when the number-crunching is well and thoroughly executed will useful information become clear; and this links firmly to point 10 below.

## 10. USE IT AND ACT ON THE FINDINGS

This simple heading is in a way the most important of all. If research is done and it is well done, then it should be used and, if it is, decisions are likely to be better. But maybe the findings are surprising, unbelievable, or unpalatable. If so, then the power of the status quo can be great. There are always a hundred ways of rationalizing the thought that the research is of no use.

While research should not remove the need for judgment, it can make a difference and should not be ignored. For example, research done by an American manufacturer of roof waterproofing materials in a European market they planned to enter, showed that the incidence of flat roofs (which is what the product was designed for) was very low – quite different from the home market in the States. In this case the timing of the research, which was designed to help target sales activity, was wrong. The company had already invested in the construction of a factory. This fact played a strong part in the research being rationalized as – *unimportant* – and the launch went ahead despite the market information. A year later the factory closed; losses were higher than they would have been if the research had led to a decision to cease operations; and much, much higher than if the research had preceded building the factory and another target market had been found at that stage.

If research is worth doing, and well done, then it is worth listening to and acting on. It may only present part of the full picture, but it is an important part.

Research is no panacea, but if well conceived and well conducted it can provide a valuable tool for any organization. Whether simple or complex, it can provide information to assist decision-making, and perhaps highlight issues that might otherwise be neglected. It enhances management judgment and makes decisions taken more likely to reduce risk and help the business grow.

# Frequently Asked Questions (FAQs)

**Q1: Market research seems to incorporate a variety of different things (product research and customer research, for instance) – just what does it encompass?**

A: Market research is both one of the individual techniques and an umbrella term encompassing more - Chapter 2 explains.

**Q2: What is the difference between market research and marketing research?**

A: See Chapter 1.

**Q3: Market research is expensive, is it worth the cost?**

A: It need not be expensive (though some studies, of course, are) - Chapter 2.

**Q4: Can market research help when my markets are spread across the world?**

A: Chapter 5 looks specifically at this and at how research conducted on an international basis is different from that conducted in one market.

## Q5: The complexities of seeking respondents to survey seems considerable, can the Internet help?

A: It is helping more and more – see Chapter 4.

## Q6: I am confused by all the technical terms (what's regression analysis for goodness' sake?)

A: There are a good many technicalities to get to grips with, Chapter 8 has a glossary listing general terms and others specific to a variety of research techniques (and, yes, there is a definition of regression analysis there too).

## Q7: What exactly does a research agency do?

A: A clear description of how they can assist is part of Chapter 6, also this is referred to at the end in Chapter 10.

## Q8: Is research affected by all the changes relating to e-commerce and the Internet?

A: Yes, it is, and a clear overview about this is set out in Chapter 4.

## Q9: Are there ethical guidelines preventing research being used in inappropriate ways (for example to disguise high-pressure selling)?

A: There are codes of practice that address this and a host of other issues; see Chapter 9.

## Q10: How exactly does a research project work?

A: A typical project and the way it needs to be conceived and organized is part of the content of Chapter 7, which also features a number of cases studies.

# Acknowledgments

I can claim no credit for the origination of the unique format of the series of which this work is part. So thanks are due to those at Capstone who did so, and for the opportunity they provided for me to play a small part in so significant and novel a publishing project.

I would like to thank my co-author Robin Birn, who runs Strategy, Research & Action Ltd, not only for his help and assistance, but for again making the process of collaboration so painless; as when we previously co-authored *Marketing in Publishing*. Though I have actually set down the majority of the words contained herein, many (most?) of the ideas and technical points represented are his; I simply could not have completed this project without his assistance. His other books on market research, which are drawn on here to some extent, are well worth tracking down and are referred to in Chapter 9.

Two specific chapters were largely contributed by others. Chapter 3, "The Evolution of Market Research," by Katherine Evans, who runs Peke Research, based in Essex; her research on the details of the history of market research was so extensive that I now worry about what space prohibited from being included. With Chapter 4, "The E-Dimension," by David Walker, international director (new media) of Research International Group. Both did an excellent job at short notice while I also worked to complete the ExpressExec title on *Negotiation*. The arrangement assisted both titles in being delivered on time. Besides, both are better sections as a result of their involvement; many thanks to both.

Thanks also to Gary Lim, of Gary Lim Associates in Singapore, who contributed case material from Asia. He was as helpful as he is hospitable when I visit his home city.

Last, but by no means least, thanks to Emily Smith, who acted as researcher searching out back-up material and references that saved me time and helped me meet a tight deadline. She took on the task at short notice and did a thoughtful, thorough, and useful job; such help is much appreciated.

Patrick Forsyth
Touchstone Training & Consultancy
28 Saltcote Maltings
Maldon
Essex CM9 4QP

Robin J. Birn
Strategy, Research & Action Ltd
Parkway House
Sheen Lane
London SW14 8LS

# Index